Morning Glory

25 Years in Edmonton: A Quarter Century of The Edmonton Sun

Published by

Acknowledgments

Publisher
Craig Martin
Editor
Graham Dalziel
Design and Layout
Barry Hanson
Proofreader
Shirley Taylor
Photo Editor
Gary Bartlett
Photo Reproduction
Brad Ray
Alex Wylie
Research
Kathy Levesque
Carol Woods
and *The Edmonton Sun*
News Research staff
Cover Art
John Fehr
Production
Will Stephani

About the Authors

KERRY DIOTTE has worked at *The Edmonton Sun* since 1985 and has first-hand knowledge of many of the stories that appear in this one-of-a-kind book.

The Sault Ste. Marie, Ont. native has worked at several key jobs at *The Sun* since 1985, including stints as a reporter, copy editor, assignment editor, news feature writer and columnist.

The veteran journalist began his career in Ontario shortly after graduating from Carleton University in Ottawa.

He worked in radio, television and newspapers in Ontario before coming west in 1982 to spend two years at *The Calgary Sun*. He then toiled for a year at *Alberta Report* newsmagazine before joining *The Edmonton Sun*.

Today Diotte works as *The Sun*'s civic affairs opinion columnist and also writes a weekly general interest column.

TERRY JONES, *The Edmonton Sun*'s highly respected sports columnist, authored *The Great Gretzky* and two subsequent Gretzky books early in the hockey player's career. He also wrote *The Edmonton Sun* books *Edmonton's Hockey Knights, 79 to 99*, and the end-of-career *An Oiler Forever*. All were Canadian best-sellers.

Jones has covered 12 Olympic Games, more than a dozen other major international Games, 11 World Figure Skating Championships and a long list of other major international sports events including World Cups of soccer and IAAF World Championships in Athletics. He's covered 30 Grey Cups, 19 Super Bowls and more than 100 World Series Games. His hockey credits include all the Canada Cups and similar events since the '74 Canada-Russia Series, and more than 450 Stanley Cup playoff games.

SUN MEDIA
CORPORATION
A QUEBECOR MEDIA COMPANY

Cover photos: Tornado photographed by Peter Cutler, taken July 31, 1987 – Black Friday; Oilers Stanley Cup celebration at Commonwealth Stadium, photographed May 27, 1990 by Perry Mah; SUNshine Girl Rochelle Loewen, photographed by Brendon Dlouhy.

Back cover photo: Rescuers free a worker trapped inside Lee Mason Tools, 6450 27 St., on Black Friday, photographed by Larry Wong.

Cover design by Graham Dalziel.

Printed by The Winnipeg Sun – Commercial Print Division

Table of Contents

Copyright The Edmonton Sun, 2003

All rights reserved. The use of any part of this publication reproduced, transmitted in any form or by any means, electronic, mechanical, recording or otherwise, or stored in a retrieval system, without the prior consent of the publisher, is an infringement of the copyright law. In the case of photocopying or other reprographic copying of the material, a licence must be obtained from the Canadian Copyright Licensing Agency (CANCOPY) before proceeding.

National Library of Canada Cataloguing in Publication

Diotte, Kerry
    Morning glory : 25 years in Edmonton : a quarter century of the Edmonton Sun / Kerry Diotte, Terry Jones, Graham Dalziel.

ISBN 0-9684526-3-9

    1. Edmonton Sun--History. 2. Edmonton (Alta.)--History.
I. Jones, Terry, 1948- II. Dalziel, Graham, 1955- III. Edmonton Sun (Firm) IV. Title.

PN4919.E343S86 2003   071'.12334   C2003-904833-0

Twenty-five Great Years!

It's been 25 years!

Naysayers did not think *The Edmonton Sun* would last 25 weeks, much less 25 years.

When the paper was born with a first edition on April 2, 1978, *Edmonton Journal* publisher J. Patrick O'Callaghan took out an advertisement in our paper to wish us "a nice visit to the city."

He was not alone in thinking we wouldn't make it.

But the army of doubters was proven wrong – dead wrong.

The newspaper not only survived, it prospered and became a must-read ritual for hundreds of thousands of people.

In the pages that follow, you will have a chance to relive many of the most fascinating stories covered by *Sun* staff in the last 25 years.

You'll revisit the major events that have shaped our city and province.

Those spectacular triumphs and catastrophic tragedies have affected all of us. They define who we are.

The Sun was there for all of them, and has carried hundreds of thousands of pictures and stories since the first edition of the newspaper rolled off the presses.

There is no way a book of this size can cover even a fraction of what has happened in and around our city in two and a half decades.

We've assembled here what we believe is a representative sample of those great, history-making events; those magical moments in news, sports and entertainment and those incredible people who have touched all our lives.

This book is not about the people who work at *The Sun*.

The edition of The Edmonton Sun announcing Wayne Gretzky's trade to Los Angeles s[...] a staggering 110,221 copies.

Newspapers spawn larger-than-life characters, and we've had our fair share over the years. Some truly were legends, while others merely thought they were. To single out a particular person for mention in this book is to do a disservice to the hundreds of other employees who have contributed to the success of the newspaper.

So while this book isn't about any of us, it is about all of us together. The stories and pictures in the book are drawn from thousands of editions of *The Sun* – The Little Paper That Grew … and grew and grew and grew!

The 1980s saw spectacular growth at the newspaper. For much of that decade, we were ranked as the fastest growing paper in the country.

On April 10, 1983, *The Sunday Sun* hit 100,000 copies sold for the first time.

There were massive sales in the years that followed.

Our best single-day sale of all time came on Sunday, Aug. 2, 1987, two days after the Black Friday tornado devastated the city. Our blanket coverage of the unforgettable disaster saw 156,528 copies snapped up.

The Sunday Sun of July 17, 1988 contained a special, full-colour 12-page supplement on Canada's 'Royal Wedding,' that of Oilers megastar Wayne Gretzky to Hollywood starlet Janet Jones. This special keepsake for fans of the

Sun photo by Robert Taylor

Toronto Sun Publishing Corp. president Douglas Creighton cuts a ribbon made up of Edmonton Sun front pages to officially open this paper's offices at 4990 92 Ave. in this April 20, 1989 photo.

couple on both sides of the border pushed sales to 138,218.

Just four weeks later, the hockey deal of the century saw Gretzky traded to the Los Angeles Kings. The Aug. 10 edition had 22 pages of pictures and stories on the block-buster deal and sold a staggering 110,221 copies.

The newspaper's dramatic growth slowed somewhat in April of 1989 when we made the necessary decision to raise the single-copy price from 25 cents to 50 cents. In the years since, the paper has posted readership gains and continues as a must-read essential for scores of loyal fans all over northern Alberta.

The '90s saw great technological change at the newspaper. We embarked on the road to full pagination early in the decade, and today The Sun is produced with top-of-the line editorial and advertising systems.

When The Sun began publishing, reporters ran around the city armed only with pencils, notebooks and a keen determination to get the story fast and first. Photographers shot pictures using film, which was rushed back to the office for processing. Reporters banged out their stories on typewriters – and copy editors using line gauges and measuring wheels manually drew up pages and sized and cropped pictures.

Things are very different today. Computers, advanced electronic publishing systems and digital cameras are the order of the day. The Sun has kept pace with rapidly changing technology, and today is one of the best-equipped and most efficient newspapers in North America.

Another milestone was reached on Sept. 17, 1994 with

the launch of the first Saturday Sun. "Finally, finally, I have a paper to read on Saturday," said Premier Ralph Klein, who attended the gala launch party at the Delta Edmonton Centre Suite Hotel. The Sun became a seven-days-a-week force to be reckoned with, offering tremendous value to readers and advertisers alike.

On July 1, 1995, we chopped about four centimetres from the depth of the newspaper to make it the 'laptop' size you're familiar with today. The reason was simple - sky-rocketing newsprint prices. Newsprint is our largest raw material cost, and reducing the size of the paper slightly meant we didn't have to pass along our higher costs to readers and customers.

The '90s also saw a number of changes in the ownership of our company. In 1994, Toronto Sun Publishing Corporation – our parent – was a subsidiary of communications giant Maclean Hunter, which was sold in a $3-billion deal to Rogers Communications Inc. Two years later, Sun staffers put together a $411-million deal to buy the Sun chain from Rogers, renaming it Sun Media Corporation.

Montreal-based Quebecor took over Sun Media in early 1999, closing a $983-million deal and taking control of 21 per cent of newspaper circulation in Canada.

This book contains many pictures and stories about people who once held titles. They were elected officials or were in the military, the police services or the church. We thought it simplest to refer to them by the title they held at the time, instead of prefixing that title with ex-, former- or then-.

Dig in and enjoy 25 years of memories.

CHAPTER ONE
Crime
and Punishment

Scores of news events have riveted the public's attention over the last 25 years.

From the kidnapping of millionaire Peter Pocklington to the slaying and sexual assault of six-year-old Corinne (Punky) Gustavson to the murderous rampage by escaped killer Daniel Gingras – there has been no shortage of gripping, headline-grabbing news.

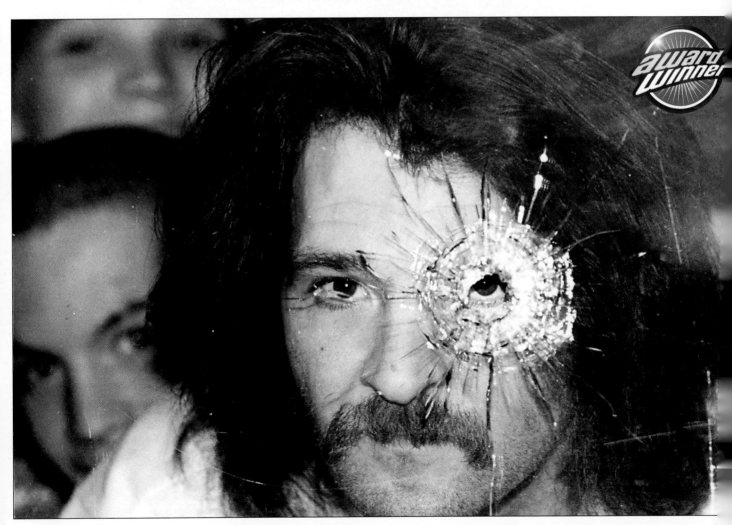

Robert Taylor caught this Oct. 17, 1994 shot of Edmontonian Claude Ransom, the apparent victim of vandalism, peering through a hole caused by a bullet shot through his window. The photo won Sun Media's prestigious Dunlop Award for Spot News Photography. Edward Dunlop was founding chairman of The Toronto Sun. The awards recognize excellence in writing, photography and editorial design.

Pocklington's Kidnap Ordeal

"I really thought I would end up in a box."

Those were the words of Edmonton entrepreneur Peter Pocklington after he had endured a tense, 12-hour hostage-taking April 20, 1982 at his Saskatchewan Drive mansion – a crime that made international headlines.

The drama began when the Oilers' owner was confronted by an armed masked man who later demanded $1 million in ransom.

It ended when city police task force officers stormed the home. Both Pocklington and the hostage-taker were wounded by a gunshot from police.

Pocklington later told *The Sun* he survived because he managed to keep his captor calm.

The businessman told how the nightmare unfolded as he walked toward his silver Rolls-Royce convertible on his way to work.

He was confronted by a masked man wielding a scary-looking .357 Magnum handgun.

He later learned the man was 29-year-old disgruntled, unemployed Yugoslav immigrant Mirko Petrovic.

Pocklington recalled: "I thought I was looking at a cannon. He said, 'Do as you're told or you're a dead man.'"

Pocklington had the gun put to his head and was led back to the house.

His wife Eva was on the phone to Pocklington's secretary and was able to tip her off when the two men entered the house.

Eva had been the original kidnapping target but the gunman's plans changed when Pocklington's wife managed to bolt to freedom.

"That really got him riled," Pocklington said.

The businessman recalls sitting with the gunman watching television. News stations were showing live coverage of police task force members gathering outside the mansion.

Pocklington said Petrovic "went into a deep shock" seeing that and "I had to calm him down again."

Eva Pocklington was assisted by one of her husband's associates as she fled the kidnapper. This spectacular picture won a National Newspaper Award for Sun photographer Robert Taylor.

7

Throughout the day police and Petrovic talked to one another as they discussed the man's ransom demands.

During those talks, Petrovic would threaten Pocklington's life or speak of killing himself.

The hostage horror climaxed when Pocklington was being led by the gunman down some stairs toward the kitchen.

The sports team owner had his hands and feet bound in wire and was being led toward a suitcase containing $1 million that had been placed in the kitchen by police.

Police stormed the place just as Pocklington leaned over to pick up the money.

Earlier, during the tense day, the hostage-taker was convinced to release two of Pocklington's staff – a cleaning woman and a babysitter.

Ordinary citizens descended by the hundreds outside Pocklington's Tudor-style mansion, standing as close as 100 metres away, shoulder to shoulder with dozens of reporters and photographers.

Pocklington later told reporters he had a lot of sympathy for his hostage-taker, who was upset about politics and the economy.

"He blamed Ottawa and the politicians," said Pocklington.

"He kept ranting and raving about Trudeau. He believed millionaires were the cause of our economic problems."

In the end, Pocklington said he got an apology from his captor.

"I was telling him how sorry I felt that this one mistake might ruin his whole life.

"He started agreeing with me. He felt sick about it. When they were taking us to the hospital, he looked over at me and said he was sorry. I believed him."

A remorseful Petrovic pleaded guilty to five charges relating to the drama. On July 23, 1982, the first-time offender was sentenced to 15 years in jail, a term the Alberta Court of Appeal later upheld.

After being paroled in April 1987, Petrovic was deported.

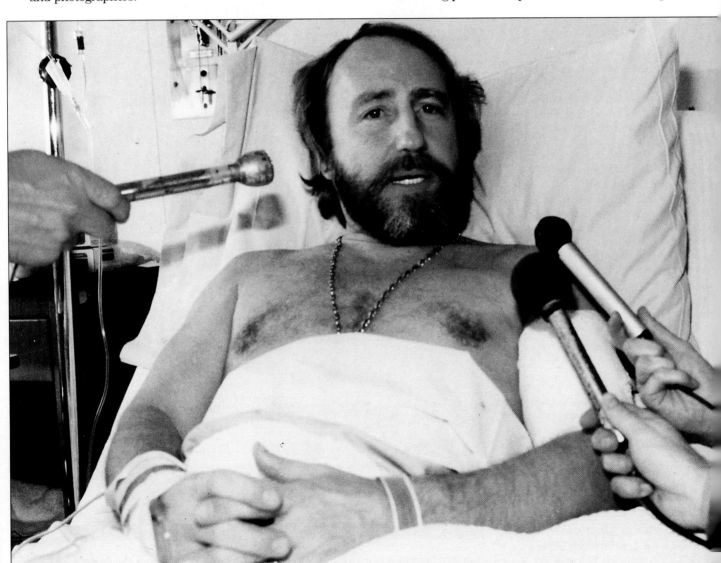

Sun photo by Gorm

Peter Pocklington was interviewed in hospital as he recovered from injuries sustained during his rescue from the attempted kidnapping.

Tania Murrell vanished Jan. 20, 1983 while walking home from school.

The Tania Murrell Mystery

The disappearance of six-year-old Tania Murrell Jan. 20, 1983 has become one of the city's most intriguing unsolved mysteries.

Tania vanished while walking from Grovenor elementary school at 10345 144 St. to the west-end home she shared with her little brother, parents – Vivian, 27, and Jack, 31 – and her beloved puppy Harley.

Within 30 minutes of Tania's failure to arrive home, her aunt and babysitter sounded the alarm.

Scores of police and volunteers hunted for her. In mere days they covered 1,900 square blocks, looking for the girl who was believed to have been abducted.

Her disappearance made headlines across North America and a haunting, smiling picture of her appeared coast to coast.

There were several cruel phone pranks that plagued the investigation, including one hatched by an Ontario man who was jailed for three years for trying to extort $40,000 for the girl's safe return.

The parents themselves faced heavy scrutiny. Talk surfaced that Jack, a carpenter, had connections with a motorcycle gang and was involved in drugs.

Both he and Vivian denied the allegations and each took a lie detector test, which they said they passed.

Sun photo by Robert Taylor

Vivian Murrell, seen here at this March 2, 1983 police news conference, said she would not wait and would start her own Edmonton drive to try to locate her missing daughter.

Sun photo by Ian MacDonald

Vivian Murrell, left, started a petition looking for army support in the search for her daughter.

Sun file photo

Vivian Murrell displays a poster of Tania in this Nov. 19, 1985 Sun photo.

TOP: Vivian Murrell with her daughter Elysia in May 1986.
RIGHT: Vivian Murrell helps Holly McQuat, 2, put her best foot forward during the Tania Murrell Finger and Footprinting service held at the Sherwood Park Mall Feb. 7, 1987. The Murrells would encounter controversy later that year over how the funds of the society named for their missing daughter were spent.

In 1987 controversy again hit the Murrells' lives.

They had moved to British Columbia after closing down the Tania Murrell Missing Children's Society, which had been launched the fall after Tania went missing.

The couple were grilled over concerns about how funds had been spent, but no charges were laid over the affair.

About 10 years after her daughter disappeared, Vivian divulged that police believed Tania was attacked and killed by a man who knew the family.

She said police told her the killer had been infatuated with the mom.

Police admitted to keeping tabs on one specific person but could not come up with enough evidence.

That chief suspect is thought to have moved to Eastern Canada and Tania's disappearance remains unsolved.

Sun photo by Peter Martin

A Loss Of Innocence

Police believe the vicious 1986 murder of Brenda McClenaghan signalled a tragic turning point for this city – a loss of innocence.

Before her slaying, virtually all murders had been so-called domestic situations where the killer and victim knew one another, police investigators said.

McClenaghan's slaying came at the hands of a total stranger.

Ironically, the tragedy unfolded after the 20-year-old college student and four friends decided to go out for a night of pure fun.

On Jan. 11, she and the others first stopped at the Purple Onion nightclub just off Whyte Avenue, then headed to a bar at the Convention Inn, 4404 Calgary Tr.

Just after 9 p.m. McClenaghan left the bar alone and was nabbed as she opened her car door by William Tame, a man with a prior conviction for a brutal rape in Brandon, Man.

Her car was found two days after she'd gone missing.

On Jan. 25, a man who'd been walking his dog discovered her frozen, naked body tied to a tree in a wooded area near 23 Street and 76 Avenue. She'd been raped and strangled.

It took an intensive police investigation before an arrest was made.

Cops had sent hundreds of letters to anyone who had

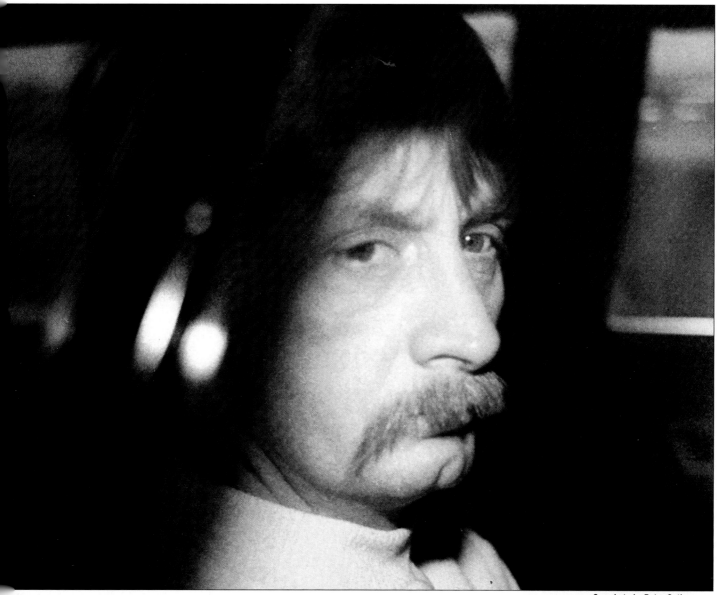

Sun photo by Peter Cutler

William Roy Tame, seen here leaving Alberta Hospital March 21, 1986, was turned in by his brother Reg, who had received a letter from Edmonton police urging anyone who had seen anything suspicious the evening Brenda disappeared to come forward.

11

Sun file photos

registered at a hotel or motel on the south side during the time of McClenaghan's disappearance.

In the letters police urged anyone to come forward if they had seen anything suspicious that evening.

Tame had stayed at an area hotel along with his brother Reg and two friends the night McClenaghan disappeared.

The room had been rented by Reg, who received the police letter. He had been suspicious of William's actions that night so he confronted him.

William eventually confessed the heinous crime to his brother.

Tame was slapped with a life sentence in the fall of 1986 after pleading guilty to first-degree murder.

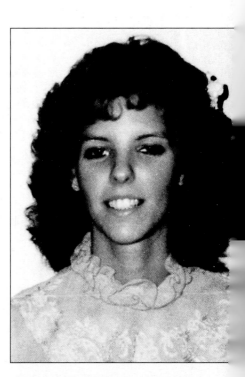

Brenda McClenaghan, a 20-year-old college student, was out with friends for a night of fun when she was abducted, raped and murdered. Her naked body was found tied to a tree, left, in a wooded area in southeast Edmonton.

The Bathtub Clue

It was a gruesome murder case that would take city police more than two years to crack.

The sordid story began innocently when young mother-of-two Susie Kaminsky sat having a drink with Roy Sobotiak and his mother Donalda Feb. 7, 1987 at a bar in the Rosslyn Motor Inn.

Kaminsky accepted an invitation to play pool at the home Sobotiak shared with his mom.

Kaminsky was never seen again.

Police suspected Sobotiak since he'd been the last to see Kaminsky alive, but it took them more than two years to crack the case.

Three days after Kaminsky had gone to the Sobotiak home police discovered her 1977 Mustang abandoned near 96 Street and 94 Avenue.

Police tried phone taps on their prime suspect but those didn't reveal anything. Nor would Sobotiak crack to his old roommate. Finally, a detective posing as a drug dealer learned the brutal truth in secretly taped conversations in September 1989.

Police learned Sobotiak had forced Kaminsky to have sex with him in the basement of his mother's home. Afterwards, he became enraged when she wouldn't consent to kinkier sex and strangled the woman who used to babysit him a decade earlier.

He stuffed her body in a duffel bag, went to his apartment and began carving up the corpse in his bathtub.

When he had done his dastardly deed, Sobotiak threw the body parts into two garbage dumpsters.

Police suspicions had become aroused in part because Sobotiak's sparkling clean bathtub was in stark contrast to his filthy apartment.

On July 11, 1991, Sobotiak, 27, was convicted of second-degree murder after more than nine hours of deliberation by a jury. A judge sentenced him to serve at least 16 and a half years before he could be released.

Susie Kaminsky, in a handout photo. Her murderer, Roy Sobotiak, had killed her after luring her from a bar to the home he shared with his mother.

A Psychopath Is Still Out There

Police suspect a psychopath killed hairdresser Melissa Letain in February 1987.

And he's still on the loose.

The 24-year-old's body was found on Valentine's Day on the ice of the North Saskatchewan River, under the Genesee Bridge, about 75 km southwest of the city.

A hangman's noose and a pair of pantyhose were found wrapped around her fully clothed body.

She had not been sexually assaulted although police believe the man had planned to do so but may have been scared off.

Letain went missing Feb. 13 as she walked on a path south of West Edmonton Mall after leaving her hairdressing job at Champs Elysee. It was a seven-block walk home and she had left work just after 9 p.m.

A witness had seen a woman matching Letain's description struggling with a man on the path near 175 Street and 87 Avenue.

Police never recovered Letain's purse, red wallet, key chain, watch or a Valentine's Day pennant she had bought for her boyfriend.

RCMP homicide Sgt. Ray Munro told journalists police suspect the person who got away with murder has a "psychopathic type of personality.

"I don't think a hangman's knot has been used in any other murder in Canada," said Munro.

Sun file photo

Hairdresser Melissa Letain was last seen struggling with a man on a path on her way home from work Feb. 13, 1987. Her fully clothed body was found the next day on the ice of the North Saskatchewan River beneath the Genesee Bridge, 75 km southwest of Edmonton.

Sun file photo

David Hansen, 28, is seen in the background as members of Marcia Charette's family comfort each other following 25-year-old Marcia's funeral in Vegreville.

A Body In The Trunk

Barroom bouncer Dave Hansen earned the nickname "The Hitman" after he single-handedly tossed two rowdy patrons from a west Edmonton bar one night in 1985.

But the nickname took on more ominous tones when the 28-year-old former rig worker was charged March 31,1987 with the murder of his fiancee's married sister.

Hansen was arrested for the strangulation murder of nurse Marcia Charette, 25, while he lived common-law with her younger sister, Julie Kuly.

The alarm was raised days before his arrest when the nurse failed to show up for her 7 a.m. shift at the Royal Alexandra Hospital.

Days later, police found her strangled body in the trunk of her car, parked at the Sandman Inn, 17635 Stony Plain Rd.

People attending his highly charged trial heard Hansen had at one time gone looking for the missing woman with her husband, Kim Charette. Hansen had also attended his victim's funeral.

During his trial, court heard Hansen testify that he and Marcia had twice slept together, including once on the day he killed her after they spent time together at a Lake Isle cabin.

He told court he choked her to death because Marcia had been criticizing Kuly.

During the trial a hushed courtroom watched a police video made in a holding room in which Hansen confessed the murder to Kuly.

"Why did you kill her, Dave?" Kuly wept as she entered the holding room. "I don't understand.

"Why did you hurt us? God, I wanted to marry you," said Kuly.

"She always said how irresponsible you are," Hansen answered, adding he and Marcia began arguing about Kuly that fateful day.

Hansen told court: "I told (Marcia), 'How do you have the audacity to sit there and tell me that Julie is this or that, when you're screwing me behind your sister and husband's back?"

Marcia Charette

Dave Hansen

That bit of testimony sparked an angry comment from Kuly who immediately yelled "liar" in court.

Crown prosecutor Gary McCuaig told court it was his theory Hansen killed Charette because he feared she might one day tell Kuly about their sexual misconduct.

That, said McCuaig, would likely have ended Hansen's relationship with Kuly.

Hansen was handed a life sentence for the second-degree murder, with no chance of parole for 10 years.

Following that, Kuly told reporters she wished Hansen could have received a death sentence.

"To me, if he took a life, he should have his life taken," said Kuly.

"I want to say on behalf of my parents and my family and everyone who supported us, that the term Dave Hansen got – a prison term – will never be justifiable in the eyes of the public or our family."

In 1989 the Alberta Court of Appeal upped Hansen's sentence to no chance of parole for 12 years. They agreed with prosecution arguments that he deserved a longer sentence because of the nature of the crime and the fact that he had a prior conviction for assault and armed robbery.

That same year Hansen tied the knot with a female minister in a behind-bars ceremony at Saskatchewan Penitentiary in Prince Albert.

Sun file photo

ABOVE: Marcia Charette's sister Julie Kuly, left, and younger sister Dallas leave court March 16, 1988 after Hansen was handed a life sentence for the murder of Marcia.
LEFT: A visibly shaken Kim Charette, Marcia's husband, leaves court March 15, 1988 after hearing Hansen testify to strangling her.

Murder And Mayhem

It began as an unlikely birthday treat for an unlikely candidate.

It ended in murder and mayhem and raised doubts about Canada's prison and parole system.

The twisted tale began June 29,1987 when convicted killer Daniel Gingras, 36, was taken from the Edmonton Institution for a day-pass birthday treat to West Edmonton Mall, largely because he was slated to get day parole by year's end.

The beefy, five-foot-10, 210-pound convict with "Murder Incorporated" tattooed on his back overpowered his unarmed prison escort and killed two people before being captured by police nearly two months after his escape.

Gingras was supposed to have been escorted by a six-foot-four bodybuilder but the con convinced officials to give him a smaller man to take him to the mall – a five-foot-nine, 52-year-old case management worker.

Shortly after the escape, prison warden Sepp Tschierschwitz spoke candidly about the birthday treat pass.

"This was his first giant step into civilization," said Tschierschwitz. "Unfortunately he screwed up."

The murders themselves were particularly disturbing.

Gingras shot rodeo clown Vital Piquette, 28, in the back of the head and dumped his body near the Edmonton Institution.

Why did he kill him? Court heard Gingras had told a girlfriend he simply didn't like the man's face.

His second victim, Wanda Woodward, 24, of Medicine Hat, was choked to death with her own shoelaces since "she was crying like a cow." Gingras had kidnapped her to use her vehicle in a robbery.

Dick Fowler, who was Alberta solicitor general, stated that Gingras's escorted pass was a "monumental screw-up."

Following the Gingras trials for murder – along with co-accused Calvin Smoker – pressure built for an independent inquiry into the day-pass debacle.

It was later revealed a prison report prior to his birthday treat pass failed to note Gingras had murdered someone after a 1978 prison escape and had a history of escape attempts.

That inquiry later raised serious questions about how the dangerous offender came to be granted a pass in the first place.

Gingras will be eligible for full parole in August 2012.

Sun file photo

Daniel Gingras, seen here in 1989, murdered two people after escaping from his unarmed prison escort. Gingras killed rodeo clown Vital Piquette because he didn't like his face.

17

A Death On Duty

It was the first time in 71 years the shadow of murder had fallen upon the Edmonton Police Service.

It came June 25, 1990 when popular 33-year-old Const. Ezio Faraone died in the line of duty while chasing robbery suspects.

The 10-year veteran of the force and member of its elite task force was blasted in the stomach and head by a shotgun-wielding robber he had confronted in an alley at 116 Avenue and 124 Street.

Police Chief Doug McNally later praised Faraone this way: "In the Edmonton Police Service we have a motto, 'To Be the Best.' I want to assure you that Const. Ezio Faraone was the best."

Faraone's former roommate, Const. Dale Brenneis, remembered his pal as being totally unselfish.

"While living with Ez, I saw him at some of his lowest points in his life," said Brenneis. "And yet at those times he would still be there for his friends if someone needed him. He would put his friends' needs before his own."

More than a year after the tragic slaying, two men were found guilty of the crime.

A jury deliberated 24 hours before finding Jerry Crews guilty of first-degree murder in the slaying.

They had heard Crews fired the fatal shots from a car, ending Faraone's life.

Crews's partner in crime, Albert Foulston, was convicted of the lesser charge of manslaughter. Both men were found guilty of robbing a bank.

Two years after the slaying, Faraone was honoured when a city park, named after the policeman, was officially opened at the north end of the High Level Bridge.

That $500,000 park features a larger-than-life-sized bronze statue of Faraone, in uniform, kneeling next to a boy.

Sun photo by Perry Mah

ABOVE: Elsa Faraone (back centre), mother of slain cop Ezio Faraone, is comforted by her son Paul and daughter Jo-Anne Quarto as they follow the casket carrying Ezio Faraone after his funeral service in Edmonton on June 29, 1990. BELOW: Police investigate the murder of Ezio Faraone. The 33-year-old Edmonton police officer was shot and killed on the job while stopping a car in an alley near 124 Street and 116 Avenue after a robbery.

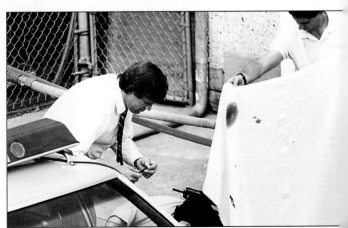

Sun photo by Dan Riec

The Killing Of Little Punky

Few crimes shocked Edmontonians more than the murder and sexual assault of six-year-old Corinne (Punky) Gustavson.

The girl went missing from the yard of her family home at Rundle Park Village, near 34 Street and 113 Avenue, on Sept. 6, 1992. Two days later, her crumpled body was found in a Strathcona County industrial yard.

She had been sexually assaulted and smothered.

Her slaying sparked the biggest murder hunt in Edmonton's history.

Cops checked out 400 suspects and more than 5,000 tips.

About 60 officers worked on the case that was featured on the U.S. TV show *Unsolved Mysteries* in 1993.

Rewards for information leading to an arrest and conviction in the case totalled $122,000.

Finally, 10 years after Punky's death, police arrested a suspect and charged him with her murder.

Clifford Mathew Sleigh, 40, was brought to an Edmonton court from Bowden Institution to face charges.

It is believed DNA evidence helped police crack the case.

Corinne (Punky) Gustavson, shown in this handout photo, was kidnapped and murdered in September 1992.

Sun photo by Dan Riedlhuber

Gustavson's body was found in this indus-rial yard in Strathcona County.

Sun photo by Jack Dagley

Punky Gustavson's coffin is carried into the Evergreen Gardens Cemetery as her dad, Ray Gustavson, her mom, Karen Vallette, her brother Barry, 7, and her sister Roseanne, 9, hug in the background.

Gruesome Discovery

Details of Jo-Anne Dickson's murder in July 1995 revolted most anyone who heard them.

Court heard Grade 10 dropout and former dishwasher Donald Smart, 26, met the 35-year-old mother of two at a pub in the Commercial Hotel on Whyte Avenue.

The two left the bar, went back to Smart's two-storey rooming house and engaged in some consensual sexual foreplay.

That foreplay soon turned deadly. Court heard the bearded Smart strangled the woman, then broke her neck with a barbell and weights.

The man had sex with her dead body three or four times before dismembering it.

Two days after she had gone missing, a torso was found in a suitcase on the banks of the North Saskatchewan River near Hawrelak Park.

A week later police announced they suspected the torso belonged to Dickson, who had been reported missing.

Despite hundreds of tips, cops could not crack the case until Smart's best friend called Crime Stoppers in January. Smart was arrested Jan. 30, 1996.

Sun photo by Dale MacMillan

TOP: Jo-Anne Dickson disappeared after meeting a man in a Whyte Avenue pub one evening in July 1995.
BOTTOM: Dickson's friend Velma Martell talks to reporters at the end of the Donald Smart trial.

Sun photo by Christine Vanzella

ABOVE: A police diver searches the North Saskatchewan River near where a torso was found in a suitcase on the riverbank in this July 20, 1995 photo. RIGHT: Donald Smart was arrested in January 1996 after his best friend called Crime Stoppers.

After his arrest Smart led homicide detectives to two or three other sites near the North Saskatchewan where he had dumped Dickson's limbs and head.

In June 1997 Smart was found guilty of second-degree murder and handed a life sentence.

In sentencing him, Judge Cecilia Johnstone ruled he would not be eligible for parole for 20 years.

Johnstone called the murder "vile ... a clearly cruel, callous and sadistic crime."

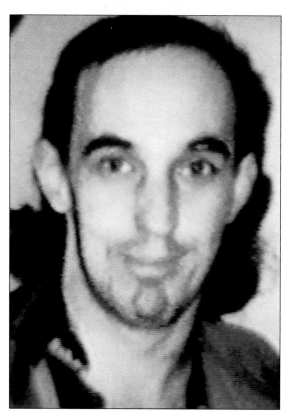

The Bizarre Tan Trial

The titillating Con Boland-Marilyn Tan story of 1995 had it all: love, hate, kinky sex and AIDS.

The story made headlines across North America after it was alleged Tan injected her ex-lover Boland with the HIV virus.

During the sexy Filipina society girl's sensational trial in May 1995, it was alleged she lured the high-society photographer to California in 1992, joined him in some sadomasochistic sex involving whips and nipple clips and stuck him with an HIV-infected needle.

She wound up being found not guilty of the attack.

Tan, who was 35 at the time of her trial, was acquitted of aggravated assault, administering a noxious substance and conspiring to administer a noxious substance.

But she was found guilty of uttering

Sun photo by Robert Taylor

ABOVE: Con Boland with a portrait he shot of Marilyn Tan in July 1993, after the allegations that Tan had infected him with HIV became public.
LEFT: Tan leaving court in May 1995. She was acquitted of all charges save one: uttering a death threat against Boland's ex-girlfriend.

Sun photo by Walter Tychnowicz

a death threat against Boland's ex-girlfriend, Jeanette Kunkel – something Tan apologized for in court.

"I just want to apologize for whatever happened with Jeanette. I didn't mean to do that ... I don't even know why I did it. I'm very, very sorry."

After the trial, Boland admitted to still caring for Tan.

"She has wonderful qualities and she's a good woman," he told *The Sun.*

Tan was alleged to have twice injected Boland, 47, with HIV-infected blood during kinky sex in spring 1992.

The photographer tested positive for the AIDS-linked virus later that year.

The case had relied heavily on the evidence of Tan's former confidante Rachel Deitch.

She had told court she helped hatch a plot to inject Boland, and claimed Tan had told her she'd later followed through with it.

Deitch also said she had obtained the tainted blood and sent it to Tan.

A Court of Queen's Bench justice discounted Deitch's story.

He said Boland's HIV-positive status was not enough proof because the photographer's lifestyle put him at risk of getting the virus from other sources.

Other high-profile Edmontonians were dragged into the court case, including wealthy financier Bruce Sansom, who tried in vain to have a publication ban on his name when he testified at the trial. Court heard Sansom, nicknamed the Fairy Godfather, carried on an affair with Tan since 1992 and offered her $2 million to stay with him.

The headlines surrounding Tan and Boland didn't stop with that lurid trial.

June Vivian, a onetime model and occasional hooker, was given a six-month conditional sentence in January 1997 for stabbing Boland in the head, neck and shoulders with a kitchen knife eight months earlier.

She had often been described as a dead ringer for Boland's notorious former flame, Tan.

During Vivian's trial court was told she was frantic at the time of the attack after mistakenly believing the HIV-positive Boland had sex with her while she slept at his Riverdale studio.

Sun photo by Perry Mah

Model Marilyn Tan leaves the courthouse with her lawyer, Sterling Sanderman.

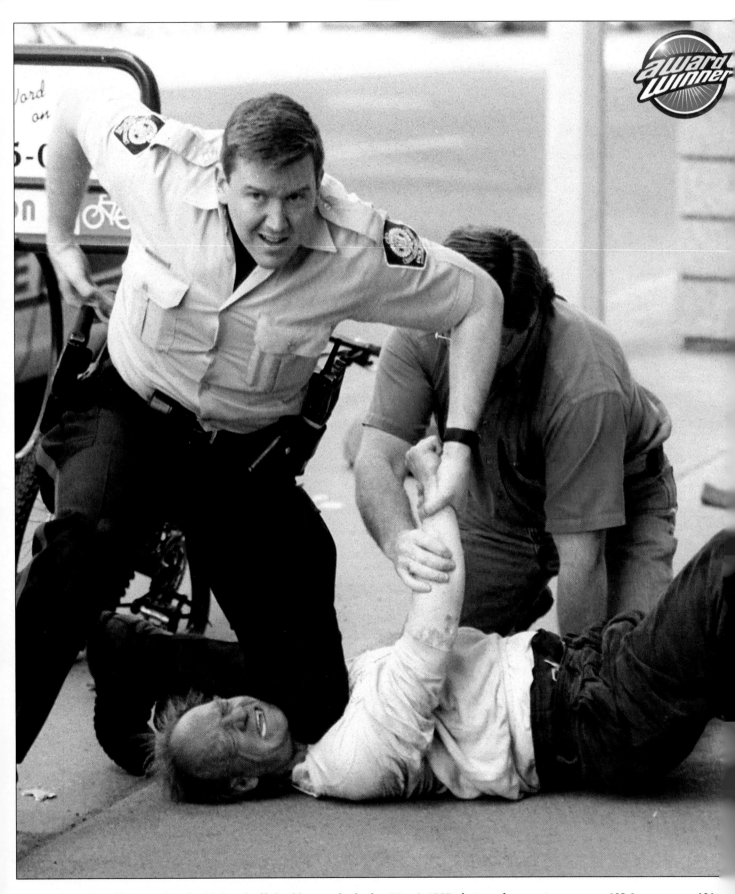

A city police officer reaches for his handcuffs in this award-winning May 8, 1995 photo as he arrests a man on 103 Avenue near 101 Street for causing a disturbance. This Walter Tychnowicz shot won a Western Canadian News Photographers Award.

The Balaclava Rapist

He was known as the Balaclava Rapist – and he struck terror into the hearts of Edmonton women from 1978 to 1983.

Larry Takahashi, who holds a second-degree black belt in karate, was notorious for attacking women in the lobbies of highrise apartments or in their bedrooms.

Wearing a balaclava was the trademark of his crimes.

Edmonton police originally suspected him in the rapes of more than 100 women, but a pre-trial deal was struck in exchange for a guilty plea.

Takahashi pleaded guilty to 14 charges in connection with attacks on seven women between November 1979 and March 1983.

Details of the crimes horrified Edmontonians:

• He raped an 18-year-old woman in the bedroom of her parents' home.

• He raped a 24-year-old woman in the garbage room of her apartment building.

• A young mother was raped in front of her infant children.

• In one violent attack Takahashi struck an 18-year-old woman repeatedly on the head. He broke her nose and permanently damaged her cheekbone.

In 1984 the 31-year-old was sentenced to three concurrent life sentences for his crimes and has since made headlines for other reasons.

Only five years after sentencing, he was granted escorted passes for leisure activities that included swimming and playing golf and hockey.

The passes were suspended after *The Edmonton Sun* wrote about his pleasure outings.

Since then he has tried in vain to obtain unescorted day passes from a minimum-security facility in British Columbia.

In 1999 Takahashi admitted to justice officials he still had violent sexual urges and fantasies about attacking females.

"A lot of things remind me of raping," he told a National Parole Board hearing.

"That urge will always be there but an urge is a far cry from coming to the point of doing it."

He has been eligible for parole since 1990.

Prior to being turned down by the parole board in 1999, one of Takahashi's victims told reporters the rapist should never go free.

"I just don't want him loose," said the woman, who called herself Sandy.

"Please, dear God, don't let him loose."

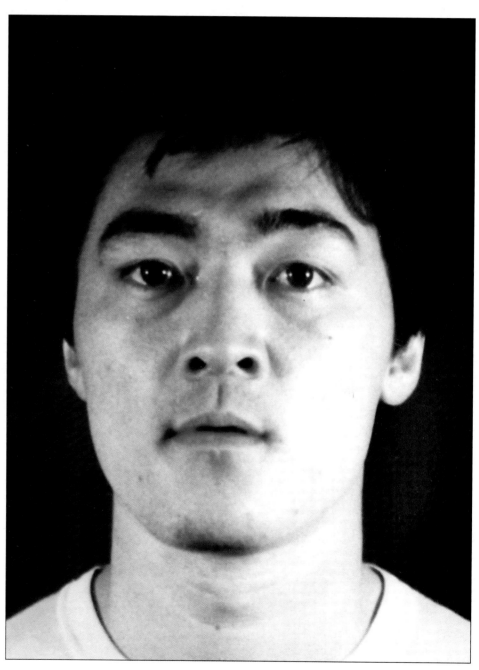

Larry Takahashi, seen in this police handout photo, pleaded guilty to 14 charges in connection with attacks on seven women between November 1979 and March 1983.

The Strange Saga
Of Jason Dix

The long and strange story of Jason Dix ended in June 2002 when he was awarded $764,863 in damages in a malicious prosecution lawsuit brought against police and prosecutors.

He'd launched the suit after spending 22 months in jail before the case against him, for an execution-style double slaying, was dismissed.

In the decision released June 17, 2002, former Court of Queen's Bench Justice Keith Ritter said the police and prosecutors in the case were "legally cloaked in malice."

Ritter slammed some police tactics as "reprehensible," including their lying to Dix and his ex-wife about his having failed a polygraph test, and breaching many of Dix's charter rights.

Tim Orydzuk

James Deiter

Sun photo by Walter Tychnowic

Jason Dix chats with the media at the Edmonton Law Courts building during a break in his case against the RCMP and provincial Crown Oct. 11, 2001. He sued police and prosecutors for malicious prosecution, after charges against him in a double-murder case seven years earlier were dismissed in 1998.

Dix sued the Crown and RCMP on Feb. 1, 1999, after murder charges against him were dismissed Sept. 3, 1998.

He'd been charged with the Oct. 1, 1994 execution-style shootings of James Deiter, 24, and Tim Orydzuk, 33, at a Sherwood Park recycling plant.

There had been shocking testimony during the Dix murder trial, including details of methods used to try to ultimately get a murder confession from the suspect.

Court heard about Project Kabaya, an elaborate operation costing hundreds of thousands of dollars in which police posed as gang members.

The operation involved Dix meeting a phoney Toronto mobster and witnessing a staged murder in British Columbia.

In handing out the settlement to Dix Ritter also slammed Crown prosecutor Arnold Piragoff for misleading a judge during a bail hearing for Dix, concerning an RCMP-forged letter purported to be from a supposed jailhouse informant.

Piragoff withdrew from Dix's 1998 murder trial after being accused of misleading the court by misrepresenting the police-forged letter.

"To knowingly mislead a court is grave misconduct," Ritter said.

Sun photo by Gorm Larsen

RCMP search dump bins in this Oct. 3, 1994 photo near the paper recycling plant where James Deiter, 24, and Tim Orydzuk, 33, were killed.

Walter Tychnowicz captured this July 2, 2001 shot of riot police attempting to arrest a man as authorities started moving in on a crowd of post-Canada Day rioters on Edmonton's Whyte Avenue. This photo won numerous awards, including a Sun Media Dunlop Award, and was a finalist in the National Newspaper Awards.

CHAPTER TWO

Disasters, Tears and Tragedy

It was a day that came to be known as Black Friday.

On July 31, 1987 a devastating tornado ripped through Edmonton and area, killing 27 people, injuring hundreds and causing $330 million in property damage.

That was just the most memorable of dozens of terrible tragedies that filled the pages of The Sun in the last 25 years.

Few people will ever forget other calamities, including the February 1986 Hinton rail disaster and the March 1985 crash of two C-130 Hercules aircraft that snuffed out the lives of 10 military men.

In this Sept. 25, 1993 photo by Walter Tychnowicz, people fleeing a nighttime fire at a downtown apartment building are assisted down a ladder by firefighters. This image earned a Sun Media Dunlop Award for Spot News Photography.

The Great Escape

For a time on March 3, 1979, nearly everyone in Edmonton held their breath.

Almost 20,000 residents of southeast Edmonton were forced to flee their homes in what was the largest evacuation of people in this city's history.

The residents, mainly from Mill Woods, took refuge in schools, hotels and community halls after an estimated one million litres of propane gas leaked into the city's sewer system in the southeast.

Just before 12:15 p.m. that day a truck driver drove over a pool of propane gas that had leaked from a damaged pipeline near 12 Avenue and 40 Street.

Heat or sparks from the vehicle sparked an explosion and blaze. The driver escaped, badly burned but alive, but the flames from the fractured pipeline below shot into the air. Emergency crews also had to deal with a series of smaller related explosions and fires.

Thousands were then forced to evacuate the area as the gas leaked into sewers, turning them into potential bombs.

It was nearly 24 hours following the initial explosion before residents were allowed to return to their homes, after city crews flushed the gas out of the sewers.

When residents returned and breathed sighs of relief, they also spoke about how the scare pulled the community together.

Don Freeman, a social worker who manned an emergency shelter at Harry Ainlay high school, sang the praises of the people involved.

"It was just great to see the way people responded," Freeman said.

"It was the kind of response you would expect in a small town, but most of these people were complete strangers."

Freeman said more people

Sun file photo

Workmen examine the pit left after a propane explosion in Mill Woods March 3, 1979. Some 20,000 residents of Mill Woods and Kaskitayo fled the area because of the lethal stream of gas, which could have reduced their communities to smoke and ruins. Construction crews damaged a pipe at 12 Avenue and 38 Street that allowed propane to escape and form an invisible pool of gas. That pool ignited when a truck drove through it, setting off a blast that sent flames high into the air.

than necessary volunteered to help at the emergency shelter and when the first shift of volunteers was slated to go home at 2 a.m., instead most stayed on to help.

Sheena MacLean, a mother of two who spent the night at the school after being evacuated from her home, was touched by the kindness of strangers.

"Everybody was so kind," said MacLean. "They couldn't do enough for the kids.

"This sort of thing is a very frightening experience, but when you see the way people stop thinking of themselves and help out it almost makes you glad these things happen now and again."

A subsequent probe into the gas leak spread the blame around. The Energy Resources Conservation Board report concluded the leak was caused by construction crews damaging a high-pressure line.

But that same report dished out blame to the pipeline company and to the City of Edmonton for not monitoring construction going on nearby.

The report noted damage had been done to the line four times without pipeline operator Gulf Canada being told about it.

Even Gulf Canada got a blast in the report, for not more carefully monitoring the pipelines it operated.

– Sun file photo

embers of the work crew who battled to stop the flow of gas to the ruptured pipe survey the scene.

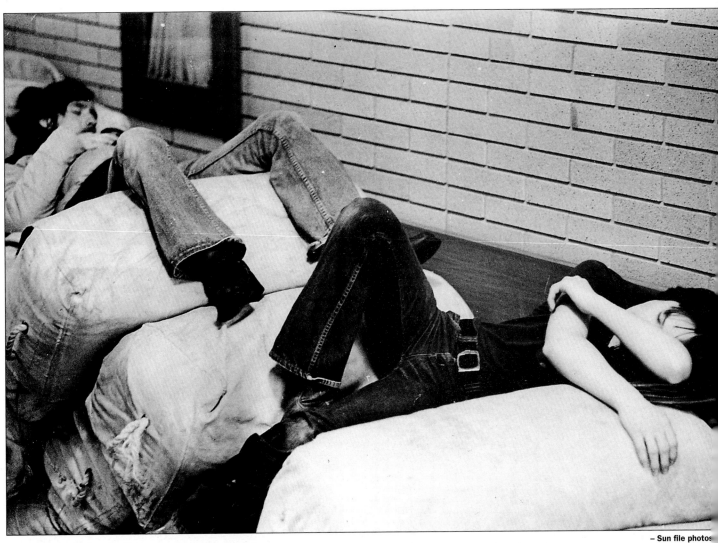

– Sun file photos

ABOVE: Two evacuated residents try to sleep on makeshift beds at Harry Ainlay Composite High School following the gas explosion and mass evacuation in Mill Woods. About 600 people spent the night in three south-side schools.
RIGHT: The explosion tore open the broken pipe, causing propane to flow into the sewer system where it posed an explosive hazard. Firefighters checked the sewer for propane, which they then flushed out of the system.

Sewer Horror

It was a freak accident and a mother's worst nightmare.

Ten-year-old Stephen Clarke was sucked into a city sewer in June 1983 near his Mill Woods home.

The tragedy happened after heavy rain blew off a manhole cover on Millwoods Road. The boy had been wading in metre-deep water nearby and was sucked into the sewer by a whirlpool above it.

Police spokesman Const. Ian MacKechnie said the boy had little chance for survival, pointing out the lad tumbled eight metres to the bottom of the sewer before being swept into the nearby main line.

Due to heavy water pressure, Clarke was then pushed at least eight kilometres through the system and deposited into the North Saskatchewan River.

The tragedy came after the city was hit by a flash flood, with 77 millimetres of rain in less than 36 hours, that blew off an estimated 100 manhole covers.

"It was horrible," said Clarke's neighbour, Joe Lallh, 45, who watched the nightmare unfold. "There was nothing anyone could have done. It happened so quickly. He didn't cry out. He just vanished."

The same flash flood poured water into the basements of 300 houses, closed a pair of city intersections and left hundreds of stalled, abandoned cars littering the streets.

Clarke's grieving mom, Lorraine Beaudry, was bitter the city did not move more quickly to put up barricades after the cover blew off.

"It's no good putting barricades up afterwards," said the mom, who had left her son and two other kids in the care of a babysitter the night of the tragedy. "It should have been done before my son died."

It was 10 days before Clarke's body was found in the North Saskatchewan River near Fort Saskatchewan. Some of his burial expenses were paid for by Edmontonians. They donated money when his mom said she did not have enough cash to give him a proper funeral.

Sun photo by Paul Wodehouse

Joe Lallh, seen here in this June 26, 1983 photo, watched in horror as 10-year-old Stephen Clarke was sucked into a whirlpool and down this manhole.

33

This Oct. 14, 2000 photo, of a man reacting emotionally after arriving at the scene of an accident involving members of his family on the 50 Street overpass at Whitemud Drive, won Dan Riedlhuber a Western Canadian News Photographers Award for Spot News.

Sun file photo

Wreckage from the March 29, 1985 collision of two Hercules aircraft landed on a warehouse at CFB Edmonton. The disaster killed all 10 airmen on board, and destroyed the warehouse and several vehicles.

Hercules Horrors

Personnel at CFB Edmonton remember it as their own Black Friday.

It was Friday, March 29, 1985 when a pair of C-130 Hercules aircraft collided in midair, plunged to the ground and burst into flames.

Ten airmen died instantly in the CFB Edmonton crash.

Both planes plummeted into Lancaster Park where an explosion and fire destroyed the craft, a warehouse and several vehicles. Total damage was estimated at about $50 million. A probe blamed the disaster on a "questionable" climb-and-turn manoeuvre called a battle break.

The accident report, released about six months after the accident, said the mishap was caused when the second plane in a three-aircraft formation struck the slow-moving lead Herc at the end of a ceremonial fly-past commemorating the anniversary of the Royal Canadian Air Force.

That manoeuvre, the report concluded, is risky because there is a "brief period when the preceding aircraft cannot be seen by the following craft."

After the horrific crash, the military banned the use of the manoeuvre by Canadian military aircraft.

Base commander Col. Peter DeTracey was transferred to a desk job in Ottawa in the wake of the crash.

A year after the disaster he was still haunted by it.

It was, he said, "the darkest day of my life."

DeTracey, 48, told *The Sun*: "Whenever I see any disaster on television, I relive the whole thing over again. A chill goes up my spine."

The 1985 disaster at CFB Edmonton came three years after seven airmen were killed when a C-130 Hercules crashed during a training exercise at Namao.

That crash occurred Nov. 16, 1982 when the plane overshot an area where it was to drop a cargo out of the plane's rear doors using three parachutes.

Six Canadian airmen and an American pilot on an exchange program were killed.

A report later blamed the disaster on a faulty parachute mechanism.

Through Hell And Back

Ghastly tales of almost unspeakable horror are being told by rescuers probing the twisted metal tomb holding those killed in the Hinton rail horror. (*Edmonton Sun* - Feb. 11, 1986.)

By many measures the Feb. 8, 1986 Hinton rail disaster was among the most horrifying train crashes in Canadian history.

The fiery crash occurred near Hinton when a 114-car CN freight train slammed into an Edmonton-bound Via Rail passenger train 22 km east of Hinton, leaving 23 people dead and dozens injured.

It was estimated the two trains met at an impact speed of 140 kmh. It derailed the nine-unit passenger train and 76 cars from the freight that carried grain, pipe, sulphur and ethylene dichloride, a flammable chemical.

The burning crash scene, fuelled by the chemicals and spilled diesel oil, was an unbelievable tangle of rail cars, cargo and twisted rails stacked 10 metres high and 160 metres long.

Authorities had to employ water bombers to extinguish the resulting inferno after the freight train ran a red light on the track and plunged full speed into the passenger train.

Survivors of the crash told of their horror after being trapped inside the twisted metal.

"We've been through hell and back," said Dwayne Keddy,

Sun photo by Pete

A photo of the site of the Hinton train crash shortly after it happened.

Sun photos by Doug Shanks

ABOVE: A body is removed from the crash site by RCMP members. RIGHT: This was the scene of carnage on Feb. 8, 1986 when 23 people died after a CN freight train and a Via Rail passenger train collided 22 km east of Hinton. Justice Rene Foisy's report into one of Alberta's worst rail accidents was released January 22, 1987, and called for wide-ranging changes to safety procedures.

18, who was on board the passenger train with a friend and a brother.

Keddy said he and his pals were engulfed in flames before grain poured on top of them, extinguishing the fire.

"Things started to fall on me – seats and metal," said Keddy. "I was squished. I couldn't breathe. I had an arm and a leg sticking out and my friend Perry pulled me out."

Keddy told how the trio tried to rescue a woman moments after the crash but their effort was in vain.

"We tried to pull her out and suddenly some aluminum dripped down on her hair and she went up in flames," he said.

"We just walked away. There was nothing we could do. She didn't make it.

"The people sitting right across from us didn't make it. They got trapped. There was diesel fuel everywhere and the whole car was on fire. People got caught in the fire and we just had to watch them burn."

Passenger Madan Lal Sharma, 64, recalls being tossed to the floor by the impact, thinking at first it was a minor derailment.

"This guy ran into our coach out of the dining car," said Sharma. "He was covered in blood and was screaming that everyone in the dining car was dead."

Briton Steven Day of London had been in the dome car when the disaster happened, but managed to scramble to safety.

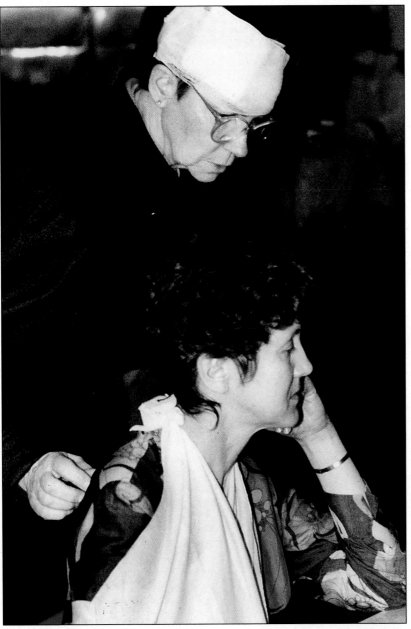

He helped a badly injured woman remove some metal from her leg.

"I lifted it off but it had cut her foot off," said Day.

"I helped carry her outside and covered her with a blanket, but there was nothing more I could do," he said.

An inquiry headed by Alberta Justice Rene Foisy blamed human error for the crash.

"The accident could have been avoided had the train crew adhered to operating rules," Foisy wrote.

"The fatigue of the train crew was a factor, as was the general poor health of the engineman," he concluded.

The inquiry heard freight train engineer Jack Hudson suffered from high blood pressure and diabetes.

The sole surviving crew member of the freight train, conductor Wayne Smith, was also taken to task in Foisy's report for failing to pull an emergency brake after he had lost contact with the locomotive engineer.

Sun photos by Peter Cutler

ABOVE: Two injured passengers, survivors of the Hinton train crash, were taken to Edmonton's Misericordia Hospital.
RIGHT: The more seriously injured survivors of the rail crash were brought to Edmonton in a bus equipped with the medical facilities of an ambulance.

Mindbender Disaster

It was an amusement ride that turned deadly.

Three people were killed and one was critically injured when West Edmonton Mall's prized $6-million Mindbender roller coaster derailed June 14, 1986.

Stunned eyewitnesses recalled the drama that unfolded that night when a car on the roller coaster jumped the track and smashed into a concrete pillar.

It occurred as the four-car, German-built train approached a loop at a speed of nearly 100 kmh.

Eyewitness David Fontaine said he heard screams and looked up to see sparks coming from the back wheels of the coaster.

"It was the worst thing I've ever seen in my life," said Fontaine. "The car just exploded."

He told how he witnessed two people plunge to the floor from the rear car and heard those still aboard the coaster screaming. It took more than 20 minutes to rescue the remaining passengers, some of whom had minor injuries.

Killed in the crash were Tony Mandrusiak, 24, who had been taking night courses in hopes of becoming a paramedic.

Mandrusiak died along with his fiancee, Cindy Sims, 21, who worked as a dental hygienist.

The third victim was David Guy Sager of Calgary.

A fourth person in the rear car, Rodney Chayko, 25, plunged about 45 metres to the concrete floor below and survived, but shattered his legs, broke ribs and a shoulder and punctured one of his lungs.

In the days that followed the accident, investigators revealed it was caused by the wheels falling off the rear car of the coaster.

A subsequent inquiry blamed a manufacturing defect in the vertical axle assembly that did not conform to the specifications of its designer.

The board of inquiry concluded the defects could be rectified, which would allow the roller coaster to safely operate again.

After correcting those defects, the amusement ride reopened in August 1987 and continues to operate today.

Sun photo by Robert Taylor

The body of one of the victims lies on the ground under the Mindbender roller coaster after a car came off the tracks and crashed into a concrete pillar at West Edmonton Mall, June 14, 1986.

Police photographers take photos at the scene of the roller coaster accident.

Sun photo by Peter Cutler

Water, Water Everywhere

In July 1986 people in north-central Alberta, including Edmonton, were bailing out after a horrific series of floods.

Hundreds of homes near the banks of the North Saskatchewan and Pembina rivers were affected by rising water levels and more than 100,000 acres of farmland were affected.

In Edmonton, the July disaster, brought on by heavy rains, affected 400 homes in the river valley, the worst flood in the city since 1915.

The North Saskatchewan River rose to a peak of 12 metres during the height of the flood, rising in just two weeks from a far more normal level of four metres.

Most of the flood damage occurred to homes in the neighbourhoods of Rossdale, Riverdale and Cloverbar.

At the flood's peak, police ordered the evacuation of 900 residents and utilities to the three neighbourhoods were shut off.

Most people refused to leave, fearing if they did so it could leave their homes vulnerable to looters.

Amos Skinner, 74, was typical of those people who employed pumps and sandbags to battle the rising water inside and outside their homes.

"We're not in danger of our lives," he shrugged from his home at 87 Street and 101 Avenue. "If I were to move, there would be looting."

The high water forced the city to shut down parks and recreation areas in the river valley, including Hermitage, Laurier, Rundle, Emily Murphy and Dawson parks, the Muttart Conservatory and the Victoria Golf course.

A mid-afternoon concert by Platinum Blonde, slated for John Ducey Park, was cancelled due to fears of flooding at that stadium.

After the flood, city crews had to deal with cleaning up mounds of silt left on roads as well as repairing buckled pavement and fixing sinkholes.

Sun file photo

These three canoeists found themselves at eye level with street signs at 101A Avenue and 87 Street in this July 19, 1986 photo.

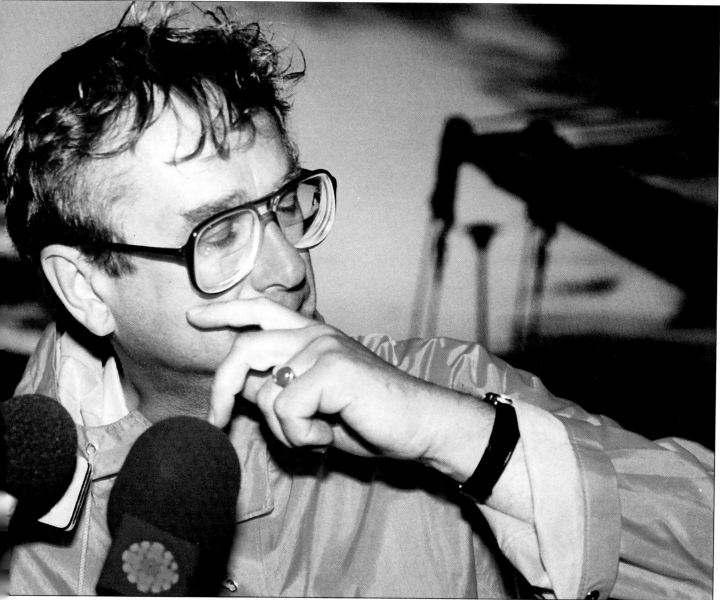

Sun photo by Jack Dagley

Mayor Laurence Decore wipes away a tear as he tries to describe a dog barking in the rubble of the Evergreen Mobile Home Park. The park was devastated when the twister hit it, after cutting a path of destruction that started in the southeast part of the city.

Edmonton's Blackest Hour

The July 31, 1987 Black Friday tornado will long be remembered as the darkest day in Edmonton history.

When the events of that bleak day ended, 27 people were dead, hundreds of others were injured, at least 750 families were homeless and property damage reached $330 million.

Forty-four-year-old pharmacist Tom Taylor was the first to spot the twister.

Edmontonians had sweltered for days and were preparing for a long weekend when the inconceivable tragedy struck.

Taylor spotted a strange cloud formation hovering about five kilometres southwest of his Leduc-area farm.

"The main cloud had wisps going around it," Taylor recalled. "Suddenly I saw a narrow funnel drop right to the ground, kicking up dust in all directions."

At 2:59 p.m. that Friday, Taylor was on the phone to the weather office giving the first warning of what would be the worst natural disaster to hit Edmonton.

After briefing weather officials Taylor dashed up to his loft to get a better look and watched breathlessly as the bizarre cloud passed menacingly overhead, heading toward Edmonton.

Minutes later he saw the funnel touch down again, six kilometres on the other side of his farmhouse. It had grown 10 times in size.

"When I saw how fast that funnel had dropped it was as if somebody had flicked on a switch and turned on the power to a giant vacuum cleaner."

An hour after his warning the tornado had steamrollered

41

an unbelievable path of destruction and death in Beaumont and southeast and northeast Edmonton.

The terrible twister battered farms just east of Mill Woods, then moved with savage speed into that neighbourhood, flattening homes and heavily damaging others.

It spun north to the southeast industrial area, crossed the Sherwood Park Freeway, then unleashed its wrath on Refinery Row, wiping out an estimated 50 to 60 businesses and leaving behind a deadly soup of spilled chemicals.

The neighbourhood of Clareview was next to feel the fury after the twister crossed the North Saskatchewan River. Three homes were flattened and a dozen others suffered heavy damage.

But the most vicious battering was reserved for the 1,700 residents of Evergreen Mobile Home Park in the city's northeast.

Fifteen of the residents were killed including four members of one family. Arlene Reimer's story was the most tragic of all. She lost her entire family to the terrible twister, husband Marvin, 40, daughter Dianne, 13, and 11-year-old twins, Darcy and Dawn.

Ten years after the tragedy Reimer told *The Sun* she still struggled.

"I just try to make it through the birthdays," she confided. "It's tough around those times. Sometimes I can't do anything then."

Evergreen looked as if a powerful bomb had been dropped on it. More than 200 of the 600 trailers were destroyed or damaged, including 91 that were flattened outright.

But there were stories of heroism and miracles in the wake of the twister.

One Evergreen victim, Kelly Pancel, 18, was killed protecting her four-week-old daughter Meagan. Pancel and two other adults put the baby between them when the twister hit.

It was bittersweet news for Meagan's father, 22-year-old Louis Pancel who declared, "My daughter is alive today because of the unselfishness of my wife. She gave her life for our child."

Mary Grandish, 27, was counting her blessings after her Clareview home's roof was ripped off by the tornado. It collapsed walls and carried off most of the furniture.

She and family friend Ron Madarash searched feverishly for her infant son Cody who had been in his crib.

There was no sign of the crib, but she and Madarash braved wild winds and torrential rain to finally spot the baby on the floor of what was left of the master bedroom.

Sun photo by Tom Bra

Little is left of the Grandish home in Clareview.

Cody was silent and bleeding, but survived.

Afterwards she declared, "He's my little miracle baby. I can't believe he lived through this."

If there was something positive out of the dark day it was the way residents of Edmonton and area came together to provide relief for victims.

Thousands of people assisted in rescue and relief efforts. They donated clothing, shelter, food and money so victims could rebuild their lives.

Because the tornado made international headlines, relief poured in from across North America and other parts of the world.

Millions of dollars were raised to assist people of Edmonton and area to rebuild their lives after that blackest of days.

Sun photo by Tom Braid

Cars were tossed like children's toys, ending up as twisted wreckage.

Sun file photo

The Black Friday twister left a path of devastation in the Evergreen Mobile Home Park.

High Arctic Heroes

Military pilot Capt. John Couch was hailed as a hero for keeping injured passengers alive after the November 1991 fiery crash of a C-130 Hercules in the High Arctic.

Five crew members died when the Herc crashed in a snowstorm just 20 km short of its destination of Alert, N.W.T., 3,600 km northeast of Edmonton.

For nearly two days 13 survivors huddled inside the plane's tail section, waiting for rescuers who could not parachute into the area for 32 hours because of a raging blizzard.

Even then, the rescuing paramedics who parachuted to the site put their lives in danger, jumping out of choppers from a mere 210 metres above the snow-covered ground.

The injured – suffering from burns, broken bones and hypothermia – had to try to warm themselves against temperatures that dipped with the windchill factor to -60 C.

Many did not have parkas or other heavy clothing because it was lost in the crash.

Crew members had only summer-weight jackets to wear.

Couch froze to death just hours before the rescuers arrived. He had given his arctic jacket to an injured passenger and refused to take it back.

Survivors could not believe they escaped death on impact. Said Lieut. Joe Bales: "It didn't look like an airplane anymore. I couldn't believe I had survived it."

Four crew members died on impact or shortly after.

Sun photo by Gorm Larsen

Heroes in the High Arctic, from left, Sgt. Ron Burke, Cpl. Darren Darbyson, Master Cpl. Jim Brown and W.O. Fred Ritchie, celebrate their successful mission. The four men were instrumental in the rescue of 13 survivors of the crash of a C-130 Hercules.

A couple cry in each other's arms after their car flipped on 87 Avenue near 160 Street in Edmonton. Nobody was hurt. This Dan Riedlhuber photo won the 1995 Western Canadian News Photographers Association News Photo of the Year award.

Sun photo by Walter Tychnowicz

A tornado rampaged through a Pine Lake resort area July 14, 2000, wreaking havoc mainly on the Green Acres campground. Searchers descended on the lake area, near Red Deer, from Edmonton, Calgary and communities along Highway 2. The tornado left 12 dead and 130 injured in its wake.

Pine Lake Tornado

Thirteen years after a tornado ripped through Edmonton, a deadly twister devastated a lake resort near Red Deer.

The tornado hit the Green Acres resort near Pine Lake, about 20 km southeast of Red Deer, killing 12 people, injuring 130, uprooting trees and shredding trailers.

Emergency crews scrambled to the area after the twister touched down July 14, 2000 five kilometres west of Green Acres campground, where 1,100 were enjoying a week-end of relaxation.

The deadly storm dished out destruction and death for 15 km.

There were tragic tales of horror including from the grieving father of the tornado's youngest victim.

He tearfully told *The Sun* how his two-year-old son was torn from his arms by the killer storm.

"You were helpless," said Rev. Jamie Holtom, 30, who was sent airborne as the twister hit their cabin and stripped his son Lucas, 2, from his hands.

"It was a blur. The cabin just disappeared ... everything was gone."

Lucas was found dead under some wreckage by his mom, Katrina Holtom, who said the terrible storm "felt like 30 seconds of hell."

When the tornado hit, the Holtoms hid inside a cabin with family members and friends – all of them huddling in fear.

Katrina told how she held desperately to her five-week-old daughter Leah while Jamie hugged Lucas in his arms.

Both parents said it was a miracle they survived, along with Leah, with only minor injuries.

Medical personnel scrambling to the scene with air ambulances and fixed-wing planes took 88 patients to hospitals on that dark day, 30 of whom were in critical condition.

After the twister wreaked destruction the lakeside looked like a bomb had exploded. Where earlier there were rows of orderly trailers, there was now a massive field of splintered wood and debris.

What had once been a play area for children was turned into a makeshift hospital area where hundreds of bleeding and crying survivors waited for medical help.

Divers dredged the lake, seeking victims and pulling up debris.

As in the case of the 1987 Black Friday tornado, Albertans rallied to help the victims of Pine Lake.

Many raced to the scene to treat the wounded moments after the storm hit.

Others donated blood when medical officials sent out alerts about shortages. Still others shelled out cold hard cash.

One heart-warming story told how attendees of a gospel convention in Red Deer passed around takeout chicken buckets and raised $30,000 to help the victims.

On-duty and off-duty RCMP and military personnel showed up to help from Red Deer, Edmonton, Calgary, Stettler, Innisfail and Olds.

The Alberta government and its federal counterpart stitched together a $12-million relief package after the killer twister.

The aid included $3,000 for each adult and $750 for each child caught in the immediate path of the 300-kmh winds.

The package also included a $15,000 re-establishment assistance grant for 25 farms hit by the twister.

More relief was doled out, up to $5,700 for funeral expenses for those who died and assistance for ongoing counselling and emotional needs for victims.

Sun photo by Walter Tychnowicz

An aerial view of Green Acres resort at Pine Lake after a tornado touched down.

Sun photo by Perry Mah, inset photos courtesy DND

On April 18, 2002 four Canadian soldiers, members of Edmonton-based 3 Battalion of the Princess Patricia's Canadian Light Infantry, were killed when U.S. pilots mistakenly bombed their unit as the soldiers took part in a nighttime training exercise outside Kandahar, Afghanistan. Canada expressed its grief at a memorial service held April 28, 2002 at Edmonton's Skyreach Centre. The four Canadians killed were, inset from left, Sgt. Marc Leger, Pte. Richard Green, Pte. Nathan Smith and Cpl. Ainsworth Dyer.

CHAPTER THREE

Pleased to Meet You

In September 1984, tens of thousands of people in Edmonton were thrilled by a visit from Pope John Paul II – the first ever by a pontiff to Alberta.

The Pope was one of the most memorable visitors to the city. Others included cancer-fighting hero Terry Fox, wheelchair wonder Rick Hansen and royal visitors Prince Charles and Lady Diana.

Suffice to say they were all given a warm Edmonton welcome.

Pope John Paul II hugs an invalid after an open-air mass near Namao in this Sept. 17, 1984 Gorm Larsen photo. The image won Sun Media's Dunlop Award for Spot News Photography.

Terry Fox

Each year in Canada there are hundreds of charity runs in honour of Terry Fox.

Since the early 1980s thousands of people in Edmonton and area have walked, jogged, biked or used wheelchairs at the local runs to commemorate Fox and to raise money for cancer research. The one-legged Port Coquitlam, B.C., man became a folk hero in the months after he began his Marathon of Hope in Newfoundland in 1980.

His dream was to run across the nation while raising money for cancer research.

It was all the more ambitious because Fox was forced to run on an artificial leg.

He had lost his right leg to cancer when he was a teenager in 1977 and had it amputated just above the knee.

But he did not take the loss of his leg lying down.

That same year the young athlete played in the national wheelchair basketball championships in Edmonton while taking chemotherapy treatment in the city.

The next year Fox began training to run. Before he even began his Marathon of Hope, Fox had run 5,000 km in training.

His brave motto for life was a simple one.

"I just wish people would realize that anything's possible if you try," said Fox. "Dreams are made possible if you try."

He began the journey April 12, 1980 to little fanfare in Newfoundland.

His friend drove a van while Fox ran an average of 45 km per day, stopping only to eat, rest and to give speeches in various towns to encourage donations.

He had a dream to get $1 from every person in Canada for cancer research.

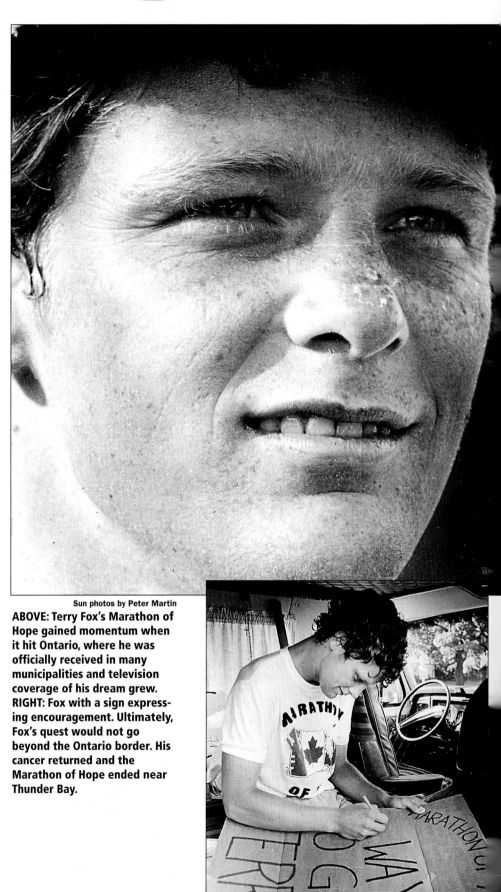

Sun photos by Peter Martin

ABOVE: Terry Fox's Marathon of Hope gained momentum when it hit Ontario, where he was officially received in many municipalities and television coverage of his dream grew. RIGHT: Fox with a sign expressing encouragement. Ultimately, Fox's quest would not go beyond the Ontario border. His cancer returned and the Marathon of Hope ended near Thunder Bay.

Sun photo by Brendon Dlouhy

Cancer survivors Mackenzie Allen, 8, left, and Miranda Klein, 21, plant kisses on the cheek of Terry's mother, Betty Fox, after an Aug. 16, 1999 proclamation at City Hall making it Terry Fox Month in Edmonton.

There was little national interest in the amazing journey until Fox hit Ontario. There he was given many official civic welcomes and was subject to intense media exposure.

Sadly, it was also the province where a big part of his dream died.

After running through southern Ontario, Fox swung to the north part of the province, hobbling through Sudbury and Sault Ste. Marie, then heading north on the Trans-Canada Highway along the rugged, hilly shores of Lake Superior.

But near the Lakehead – Thunder Bay – Fox was forced to abandon the run after 144 days and 5,377 km.

Following a medical checkup, he discovered his cancer was back. This time it had moved into his lungs.

Fox was taken back to his home province of British Columbia and died June 28, 1981 at a hospital in New Westminster, B.C.

He was awarded the Lou Marsh Trophy as Canada's outstanding athlete of 1980 and, that same year, became the youngest companion of the Order of Canada.

His dedication ultimately raised far more than $1 from each Canadian for cancer research.

Since Terry Fox commemorative runs began in 1981 in Canada, the U.S., and throughout the world, it is estimated $300 million has been raised in his name for cancer research.

Royal Pleasures

Edmontonians were royally impressed by two pairs of visiting dignitaries in the 1980s.

Prince Charles and Diana, the Princess of Wales, wowed crowds in the summer of 1983.

Four years later we were treated to a visit from the Duke and Duchess of York – Prince Andrew and Sarah Ferguson.

Charles and Diana spent June 30 and July 1, 1983 in Edmonton, in part to attend Universiade – the world student games.

Thousands of residents went gaga over the special couple, including Westin hotel general manager Steve Halliday.

He was invited into the main parlor of the 20th-floor Crown suite to personally meet the pair.

"I was a little nervous going in," Halliday said. "But once I was there they made me feel so comfortable that all of a sudden it was a very casual conversation.

"Princess Diana is just charming, she's so sweet," he told The Sun.

"And Prince Charles is so natural, so dignified. They are not affected by anything. They know how to handle themselves."

Halliday was later given an autographed photo of the royal couple.

Others who met the twosome were even more thrilled.

Lynne Filion stood in line for four hours to catch a glimpse of the couple at Sir Winston Churchill Square.

Diana shook the hand of the teen, who vowed she would never wash it again.

"She's beautiful," Filion gushed after the once-in-a-lifetime meeting.

Sun file phot

Prince Charles and Diana, Princess of Wales, did Edmonton proud when they dressed in period costume for a June 30, 1983 function at Fort Edmonton Park.

Sun file photo

The teenager had long collected magazine photos and clippings featuring the couple. "Diana was prettier than any of my pictures."

The royals attended the opening ceremonies of Universiade, dressed in Klondike gear for a function at Fort Edmonton and lunched with the lieutenant-governor. The prince also gave a convocation address for University of Alberta graduates.

It was all part of a 17-day-long Canadian visit.

On leaving, Charles told a crowd at the games: "This is our last event in Canada before we return to Britain and we shall leave here with our hearts overflowing with the warmth, friendliness and hospitality the Canadian people showered on us in the past 17 days."

Fergie and Andrew's visit came in July 1987.

Edmontonians were enchanted by Princess Di during her 1983 visit to the city for the opening ceremonies of Universiade. 'She's beautiful,' gushed teenager Lynne Filion. 'Diana was prettier than any of my pictures.'

Like Chuck and Di, they too were greeted by thousands who saw the couple do a walkabout, dress up in Klondike clothing and attend a black-tie dinner for 500.

The trip turned controversial after the couple accepted a pair of fur coats from Premier Don Getty in honour of their first anniversary.

Animal rights groups were appalled that the two accepted the furs.

The gifts made front-page headlines in London newspapers. Britain's *Sun* newspaper headlined, "Fury over Fur-gie," while the *Daily Mail* declared, "New Fergie fur coat starts row."

Getty said he did not regret giving the coats, but added, "I would never want to cause uncomfortable moments."

After their Edmonton tour, the couple headed to the Northwest Territories for a visit.

Sun file photo

The Alberta government gave the Duke and Duchess of York fur coats, a move that created controversy in the U.K. media.

Sun photo by Peter Marti

Fergie was heard to mutter an involuntary 'Cor blimey!' when she hefted her backpack in preparation for a hike in Canada's Northwest Territories.

Pope John Paul II

In September 1984 Edmonton was blessed by a visit from Pope John Paul II – the first ever by a pontiff to Alberta.

As many as 300,000 people lined the route of the papal motorcade from CFB Namao to the downtown St. Joseph's Basilica that Sept. 16, to catch a glimpse of the Catholic faith's leader.

He came here as part of a 12-day, coast-to-coast national tour he called "a pilgrimage of hope."

Many of the people lining the motorcade route had camped out on the streets for hours, waiting on souvenir stools and lawn chairs.

At several points along the route, singers and dancers from various ethnic groups performed.

Members of the city's Polish community were among the most enthusiastic. Scores of Polish-Canadians gathered on 118 Avenue to cheer their countryman when the glass-enclosed Popemobile cruised quickly down 97 Street.

When John Paul II had been Cardinal Karol Wojtyla he had visited their place of worship in Edmonton, Holy Rosary (Polish) Church.

One of the thousands of people on the route was Jan Chrzanowski, who cried tears of joy when the Popemobile passed by.

"He's so human," said Chrzanowski. "Being a Pole he remembers everybody else. He shows his heart and his human soul."

The biggest complaint about the motorcade was that it passed quickly, so people could barely get a glimpse of the holy man who was running behind schedule.

Hawkers sold papal souvenirs along the route, which was patrolled by police on foot and in the air by helicopters.

When the Pope arrived outside St. Joseph's Basilica nearly 45 minutes behind schedule, he was greeted by a thunderous ovation

Sun file photo

When Pope John Paul II came to Edmonton Sept. 16, 1984 as part of a 12-day Canadian visit, as many as 300,000 people lined the route his motorcade took from CFB Namao to St. Joseph's Basilica on Jasper Avenue.

from the flocks of people who had gathered there.

Inside, he led an interfaith service for 1,100 clergy. The only non-clergy who attended were Premier Peter Lougheed, Edmonton Mayor Laurence Decore and Saskatchewan Premier Grant Devine.

The Pope called for Christians to come together.

"The presence of Christ fills this cathedral as we praise His name and as we pray for that perfect unity among Christians," said the pontiff.

After the service, the Pope personally greeted more than a dozen denominational leaders.

Among the crowd were 15 Catholic bishops, about half from the United States.

The following day, John Paul II said mass in a large alfalfa field in Namao for a crowd estimated at between 150,000 and 200,000 people – one of the largest gatherings in the province's history.

Thousands of volunteers organized the service, including 800 medical personnel who staffed the Namao site. Many of the people attending had camped out a day earlier to get a spot near the front.

Prior to the 9 a.m. mass, in cool, windy weather, the pontiff toured through the crowd in his Popemobile for about 15 minutes, then spent about the same amount of time greeting a group of handicapped people who were in a special VIP section.

During the mass, the Pope spoke about the disparity of wealth between richer nations and poorer ones.

Said the Pope: "The poor nations ... not only lacking food, but also deprived of freedom and other human rights, will judge those people who take these goods away from them, amassing to themselves the imperialist monopoly of economic and political supremacy at the expense of others."

After the mass, the Pope delighted the flock of people, thanking them "for this solemn Eucharist in Edmonton – for the sun and the winds."

He singled out for praise the welcome he received from citizens in the streets upon his arrival.

Sun photo by Gary Bartlet

On Sept. 17 the Pope said mass for a crowd estimated at 150,000 to 200,000 people, in an alfalfa field near Namao that had been converted for the outdoor service. It was one of the largest gatherings in the province's history.

Sun photo by Peter Martin

ABOVE: Eleven hundred clergy gathered at St. Joseph's Basilica Sept. 16 to hear
Pope John Paul II. 'We pray for that perfect unity among Christians which He wills
for His followers,' the pontiff said.
RIGHT: A young boy in native dress waits for the Pope on the motorcade route.

"It was wonderful, especially the groups of singers and dancers who met me on the road."

On his trip to the area, John Paul II had intended to visit Jasper but bad weather caused a cancellation.

Instead the pontiff visited Elk Island National Park, 50 km east of Edmonton.

A park spokesman told how the Pope hiked the park, twice spotted herds of 20 bison and spent 30 minutes praying on the shores of Tawayik Lake.

When the Pope left Edmonton, he told a papal visit organizer he would like to return here.

"The Holy Father said he enjoyed his visit and hopes someday he may be able to come back," said Roy Watson, who helped to organize the papal tour.

Edmonton Archbishop Joseph MacNeil said the Pope was overjoyed with his tour stop here.

"The Holy Father was especially happy with his visit to Elk Island National Park," said MacNeil.

"He spent about two hours walking along buffalo tracks then stopped by a lake and sat down to pray.

"It reminded him of the lakes in Poland. The Pope felt right at home there."

Sun photo by Larry Wong

Sun file photo

The Pope waves from the steps of the altar at the Namao service.

Sun photo by Larry Wong

Man in Motion Rick Hansen wheels along the highway followed by supporters after crossing the Alberta-Saskatchewan border, in this Feb. 15, 1987 photo.

A Man In Motion

It was a multi-city tour that even the hardest-working rock band could never hope to match.

Wheelchair athlete Rick Hansen rolled through 34 countries.

It took him 26 months to complete his incredible 40,000-km Man in Motion tour by wheelchair.

When he ended the worldwide tour in Canada in 1987 he had raised a whopping $26 million in pledges to be used for spinal cord research.

Crossing into Alberta in February, on the last leg of his tour, Hansen was given the kind of welcome usually reserved for rock stars and royalty.

In March 1987, hundreds of people waited patiently along Highway 2 near the entrance to the city of Edmonton to get a glimpse of the wheelchair wonder who had rolled here from the East.

Almost 1,000 people cheered him at an official reception at Gateway Park.

Later, 5,000 turned up at Northlands Coliseum to hear Hansen exclaim, "It's great to finally be here in Edmonton. We've been pushing for a very long time, waiting for this moment."

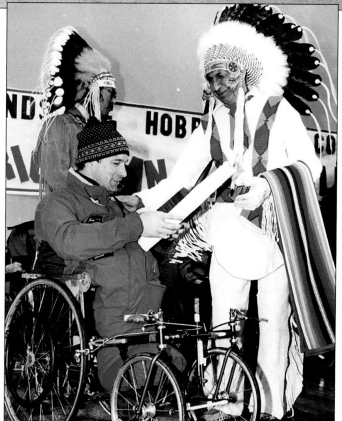

Sun photo by Peter Cutler

Hansen accepts gifts from Samson Band councillor Lloyd Saddleback during a stop in Hobbema, south of Edmonton.

The advocate for the disabled beamed as Mayor Laurence Decore presented him with a key to the city to honour his achievements.

"You've brought a Canadian awareness to a problem that needs to be better looked after," said Decore. "You are a great Canadian and a great champion."

Fans jockeyed to get an autograph from the ultimate rambling man when he wheeled around the Coliseum shaking hands.

"Oh my God," exclaimed 12-year-old Pam Mason. "I shook his hand. I thought my heart was going to stop."

Another fan, 11-year-old Robin Seymour, called Hansen, "a good athlete and gorgeous.

"A lot of people are going to realize that the disabled are just as capable as others," said Seymour.

In his oft-repeated message, Hansen told fans at the Coliseum that "the Man in Motion tour is a statement of the human spirit. It's about setting goals and chasing dreams.

"The Man in Motion tour stands for the potential of all of us to reach for our goals and to be the best that we can be."

While in Edmonton, Hansen had a whirlwind schedule of public appearances, including meetings with Premier Don Getty and several MLAs.

Sun photo by Gorm Larse

Wayne Gretzky congratulates Rick Hansen for scoring a goal worth more than $30,000 to the Man In Motion tour before an Oilers game March 7, 1987.

As hundreds of bystanders looked on, Hansen joined the Edmonton Oilers at a West Edmonton Mall Ice Palace practice. Oilers captain Wayne Gretzky presented the wheelchair wonder with a Man in Motion sketch autographed by the whole team.

Just prior to leaving the City of Champions, amid frigid temperatures, the 29-year-old thanked well-wishers for their support.

"The thing that will stay with us is not the cold temperatures but the warm hearts of the people in Edmonton," said Hansen.

Those who showed up for his early morning sendoff from Edmonton returned the compliment.

"The only way to describe him is a hero," said 30-year-old Ron Moore. "And there are not many people I would describe that way."

Sun photo by Gorm Larsen

Rick Hansen reunites with his mother, Joan Gibson, for the first time in two years, as he leaves Alberta and enters B.C.

The Bare Facts ...

Here at The Edmonton Sun while we often have our tongues in our cheeks, our cheeks are almost never on display. Sometimes, however, we just can't help ourselves.
TOP: Such was the case when we got a tip that three local Godivas would be riding horseback, nude, through the Edmonton Golf and Country Club. Imagine this golfer's surprise when the cheeky trio rode by. This May 14, 1994 photo ran in papers around the world.
BOTTOM(S) LEFT: We ran this photo of Brenda Coulombe and Dan Kowalchuk, both of Regina, on Aug. 4, 1996. They were at the Helios Nudist Association grounds near Tofield for the Western Canadian Association for Nude Recreation convention.
BOTTOM RIGHT: When University of Alberta Students' Union election candidate Kelly Shinkaruk decided to bare all – sort of – in 2002 for her campaign poster, she hit the news and the pages of The Edmonton Sun in this March 3, 2002 photo. The picture accompanied a story on the controversy surrounding her decision to use the poster.

Sun photo by Jack Dagley

Sun photo by Christine Vanzella

Sun photo by Perry

CHAPTER FOUR

We've got SUNshine

They have been movie stars, professional models, housewives and girls next door. They have been photographed in studios, outdoors, in malls and in exotic countries.

At least two (that we know of) have not been women at all.

They are the nearly 9,000 SUNshine Girls who have graced the pages of *The Edmonton Sun* since Day 1.

"It's always been one of our most popular features," says photo editor Gary Bartlett.

"You get a lot of people who collect the photos or put them up in their office."

The SUNshine Girl feature was instituted on Day 1 in *The Sun* while the SUNshine Boy first appeared a few months later.

Both features tend to get the most amount of feedback that's printed in *The Sun* – especially the SUNshine Boy.

Why?

Sun photographers think female readers have more wide-ranging tastes in men and the women aren't shy about letting our editors know if a male modelling for the photo isn't to their individual liking.

"You tend to get a lot of women calling to say 'We

Sun Photo by Brendon Dlouhy

Playboy magazine cover model Rochelle Loewen first graced The Edmonton Sun's pages as a SUNshine Girl June 17, 1998.

want younger SUNshine Boys.'

"Then when you run younger guys other women call to say 'We want more mature SUNshine Boys.' "

Bartlett says most women are almost unanimous, however, in wanting male models who shed their business suits to show off their taut bodies.

"The trouble is guys tend to be more shy than women in front of a camera. Some of them probably get teased at the office if they wear swimsuits."

Our very first SUNshine Girl, Donna Hood, says she still remembers the whole experience fondly, although it reminds her how the years have passed.

"Little did I know that being a SUNshine Girl would mean I'd get called every few years to comment on your paper," laughs Hood, who went on to become a model and actress (and later a realtor) before moving from Canada in 1995 to live in the British Virgin Islands in the Caribbean.

Oh yes, it's not normally *Sun* policy to let men appear as SUNshine Girls although two of them once did as an April Fool's joke. Ad Services Manager John McKinley, and Pat Harden, who was publisher in the '80s, both appeared in drag looking less than gorgeous.

Lynn was the SUNshine Girl of the Month for October 1993. Quite often a hint of glamour creeps into the SUNshine Girl photos, and it's no secret why. It's not unusual for the women who grace the SUNshine Girl pages, like Lynn, to be internationally known models.

Sun photo by Dan Riedlhuber

Sun photo by Bill McKeown

ABOVE: Donna Hood was The Edmonton Sun's first-ever SUNshine Girl – her photo ran in the April 2, 1978 edition of the paper. RIGHT: Doe-eyed Cheri, a hairdresser, was voted Reader's Choice as the favourite SUNshine Girl in August 1978.

Sun file photo

Sun photo by Dan Riedlhuber

One old saw suggests 'The more, the merrier' and we here at The Sun tend to agree. Over the years we've featured a number of sibling combinations on our SUNshine Girl pages, like Basia, left, and Kasia, a couple of bartenders who, in March 1996, wanted to wish their dad a happy Father's Day.

Sun photo by Peter Martin

Carol was one of the early successful SUNshine Girls, selected by Edmonton Sun readers as the SUNshine Girl of the Year for 1982. As readers can see, it didn't take long for the paper to begin running SUNshine Girl photos in colour as often as possible.

Sun photo by Dan Riedlhuber

In today's society the words 'bathing' and 'beauty' go together like ham and eggs, so it's no surprise many of our SUNshine Girl photos have an aquatic theme. Computer programmer Niki posed for this photo in September of 1999.

Sun photo by Walter Tychnowicz

Rebecca, an avid outdoors person and barefoot water-skiing fanatic was another one of our natural beauties, appearing as a SUNshine Girl in the July 27, 1998 edition of the paper.

Often, our SUNshine Gi
pose to promote an eve
the city. In this case Jar
wanted to surprise her
boyfriend and to invite
readers to a billiard
tournament at the Sha
Conference Centre, in t
April 1998 photo.

Sun photo by Dan Riedlhuber

Sun photo by Jack Dagley

TENNIS, ANYONE? ... Sports is The Edmonton Sun's bread and butter, so it's probably no surprise to regular readers to see that theme pop up in our SUNshine Girl photos from time to time. On this page, Christina, SUNshine Girl for the Dec. 12, 1996 edition of the paper, accessorizes herself with a tennis racket, though the rest of her outfit may not fulfil local tennis club regulations. NEXT PAGE: Sometimes the sports theme takes the form of booster-ism, as in this May 1997 photo of 1997 SUNshine Girl of the Year Gina, whose outfit was designed to express her wishes of success for the Edmonton Oilers.

Sun photo by Tom Braid

SEASON'S GREETINGS! … Everybody's got to start somewhere and for Erin, SUNshine Girl of the Year for 1994, it began with the photo on the right, which won her SUNshine Girl of the Month honours for December 1994. It's not unusual to see holiday themes on the SUNshine Girl and Boy pages, as Sun photographers often take the season into account when designing a shoot. BELOW: Sometimes the theme isn't as obvious, as in this photo of Steve, SUNshine Boy in the March 17, 1998 edition of The Edmonton Sun. He's Irish, and wanted to wish Sun readers a happy St. Patrick's Day.

Sun photo by Deb Unrau

Sun photo by Dan Riedlhuber

Sun photo by Dan Riedlhuber

SUNshine Girl of the Month for May
1996, Lori, another of our aquatic
models, is proof that a dark tan is not
a prerequisite for beauty.

74

CHAPTER FIVE

Movers and Shakers

Edmonton is all grown up today after 25 years of progress.
Since 1978 our city has built Canada's biggest football stadium, an NHL hockey arena and a state-of-the-art light rail transit system.
But there have been bumps along the way.
Few people will ever forget the collapse of local financial empire the Principal Group or the ugliness of the Gainers meat-packing plant strike that preceded the closure of the facility.

Picket Susan Dobbs is run over during a strike at an Edmonton engine rebuilding shop. This March 29, 1994 photo from Walter Tychnowicz won a Sun Media Dunlop Award for Spot News Photography.

Biggest In The Country

Construction began in December 1975 on one of Edmonton's most visible monuments – Commonwealth Stadium.

The 54,000-sq.-ft. facility cost a relatively modest $21 million to construct, in time for the 1978 Commonwealth Games.

The facility, employing a similar design to one used by the Iowa State University stadium, was given the go-ahead by Edmonton city council in August 1975.

The first crowd to enter Commonwealth numbered 20,000. They flocked to see the new digs, which featured a state-of-the-art $150,000 sound system.

The stadium's first spectators were wowed by the facility and happily chugged scores of soft drinks and juice to wash down the 75-cent hotdogs. Beer was not allowed in those early days. The biggest complaint from the first customers was the fact that people could not buy ice cream, chocolate bars, hamburgers or cigarettes at the concessions.

Commonwealth's original seating capacity was only 39,384 but was later drastically expanded.

Today it has a seating capacity in excess of 60,000 and is Canada's largest stadium.

As many as 17,000 people can be seated on the playing field for concerts and other events.

In 1979 there was push by some to see a roof built on the open-air stadium.

A city council report in 1979 from the parks department revealed it would cost $47 million to install an inflatable roof – more than double the cost to build the original structure.

In the report, city officials said the only way that roof would make economic sense was if the stadium hosted 120 events each year, attracting more than 20,000 spectators to each event.

The inflatable roof plan fizzled.

Sun photo by Petr Honc

Months before the first major event was held, Commonwealth Stadium was already recognizable as the venue that today serves as the home field for the Edmonton Eskimos, a site for major rock concerts and the focal point for world-class sporting events.

Sun photo by Bill Brennan

Mayor Cec Purves gets a helping hand from Judy Ripley, left, and Jeanne Ratcliff after driving a light rail transit engine through a paper barrier in October 1980 to mark the beginning of construction on the Jasper Avenue extension of the LRT.

A Big-league City...

When Edmonton's light rail transit (LRT) system opened in April 1978 it did so with much hoopla.

Officials proudly noted the system would efficiently move people to that year's Commonwealth Games in Edmonton.

People were pleased that a five-kilometre chunk of the original line from downtown to the north side was built underground – just like a big-city subway system.

Edmonton's LRT system in 1978 – successful beyond all expectations.

An initial five-station section from downtown to the Belvedere station was built in four years at a cost of $65 million.

When it opened in late April 1978 a news story in *The Edmonton Sun* boasted: "Edmonton officially joined the ranks of big-league cities yesterday when its first subway line was opened..."

Even in 2003, when the LRT's 25th birthday was celebrated, city head honchos boasted in a media release about the fact a small community operated such a system.

"Edmonton was the first city in North America with a population of under one million to build a modern light rail transit system."

That fact has also plagued the system's development over the years, since it has been more expensive to build than originally imagined and less heavily utilized.

As of summer 2003 the city had spent $350 million for the one-line, 12-km, 10-station LRT system that extends north from the city's downtown to Clareview.

A good chunk of that cost came because of the choice to tunnel both downtown and underground at the University of Alberta.

Sun photo by Peter Cutler

City employees Richard Ostrowski, left, Ivan Jerebic, centre, and John Jaksitz break open a couple of bottles of bubbly to celebrate the completion of an 800-metre stretch of tunnel to extend the LRT line past Government House and south to the North Saskatchewan River. The breakthrough in the 15-month project came at 2 a.m. Dec. 9, 1987, under 109 Street and Jasper Avenue.

The city's next move is to spend about $100 million to take the LRT line from underground at the University of Alberta to the surface, and extend it 640 metres to what will be the Health Sciences Station.

The plan is to then slowly extend it about eight kilometres south to Heritage Mall, 2323 111 St., at a cost of $522 million.

Once completed the city will have spent nearly $1 billion on the 20-km-long, one-line system.

By contrast, Calgary built a 29-km, three-leg, 31-station LRT system for $550 million, largely because officials decided to build all of it on the surface.

The payoff for them? Calgary's system provides 150,000 rides a day compared with 40,000 weekday rides here.

The other big worry with future LRT expansion is one that politicians – including present Mayor Bill Smith – freely admit.

There is no long-term commitment of financing from the province or the feds. The city is using provincial gasoline tax money to pay the bulk of the latest $100 million in construction.

By summer 2003 the federal government had pledged a mere $8.6 million for some of the future work.

It is thought, though, that since the Grit government passed the Kyoto accord, there could be more funding down the road.

The accord means Canada must begin cutting emissions of greenhouse gases – something that can be achieved in part by increased LRT construction.

Sun photo by Keith Zukiwski

ABOVE: PCL-Maxim crews construct the $14-million, six-pier LRT bridge over the North Saskatchewan River in this July 31, 1989 photo.
BELOW: A band of Scottish pipers and Mayor Cec Purves were on hand at the official opening of the Clareview Transit Station in April 1981.

Sun photo by Carmen Bankonin

Sun photo by Larry Wong

Ald. Olivia Butti 'launches' the galleon in Phase III of West Edmonton Mall during the official opening in September of 1985.

West Edmonton Mall Phase III

The superlatives were flowing as freely as the champagne when Phase III of West Edmonton Mall opened.

An estimated 100,000 people showed up Sept. 10, 1985 to marvel over a massive expansion of the one-of-a-kind mall and entertainment complex that first opened in 1981 with 220 stores and services.

The Phase III expansion saw the addition of hundreds of stores and services, an indoor theme park, a waterpark with a 12.7-million-litre wave pool and the Deep Sea Adventure attraction featuring underwater rides in four miniature submarines capable of diving as deep as 46 metres.

The owners of the mall – four Ghermezian brothers and their father – repeatedly crowed that the Phase III expansion

made the facility the eighth wonder of the world.

Most of the people who showed up the night of Phase III's opening were duly impressed at the sheer size of the ballooning behemoth.

"It's as big and impressive as the Ghermezians said it would be," gushed Mayor Laurence Decore after he watched as a celebratory bottle of champagne smashed against the hull of a full-sized replica of Christopher Columbus's ship, the Santa Maria.

Shoppers who showed up for the opening seemed awestruck by the sheer size of the place.

Jack Landalls, visiting from Winnipeg, was stunned at the king-sized complex.

Said Landalls: "This makes you think. Why don't they cover the whole of Canada under a dome?" The city's fire marshal, Robert Kotash, was less enthused about the grand opening because it was overcrowded with people, he claimed.

He said the crowd of 100,000 was far too big for the area they had squeezed into, and most could barely move.

Had there been any panic, said Kotash, there could have been "many people seriously injured and perhaps a number of people would have been killed."

A WEM spokesman admitted the overcrowding happened because about 40,000 people, who weren't invited, crashed the party.

A year after Phase III was added, the megamall was expanding again with the addition of the Fantasyland Hotel boasting 354 rooms, 105 of which were decorated in themes, including Roman rooms and Polynesian rooms.

Phase IV in October 1998 saw the gigantic mall and entertainment complex add a luxurious multi-screen cinema and an Imax 3-D theatre, as well as a second hotel, taking the whole complex up to 5.3 million sq. ft.

The superlatives have continued to flow liberally ever since.

It is far and away the world's biggest mall and indoor entertainment complex, occupying a 48-city-block space that is the size of 104 Canadian football fields.

It features 800 stores and services, 59 entrances and parking for 20,000 vehicles.

It is said to have the world's largest indoor lake, theme park, wave pool and bungee-jumping tower.

West Edmonton Mall has been called a small city – and like any community there have been tragedies despite its corporate mission statement promising "a safe and friendly environment."

At least six people have died of unnatural causes at WEM, including three in the 1986 crash of the Mindbender roller coaster.

Two people have drowned at the Deep Sea Adventure attraction, including a scuba diver doing maintenance and a bar patron who went for a fatal late-night swim.

One person was stabbed to death as shoppers looked on in horror.

West Edmonton Mall owners plan a further $145-million expansion over the next 10 years that will include a 12-storey office tower, a 12-storey apartment building, an 8,000-seat multi-use arena and a 22% boost in retail space.

Sun photo by Doug Shanks

Marcel Cardinal, 13, carries some of the 500,000 helium-filled balloons that were part of the gigantic opening of West Edmonton Mall's Phase III.

Sun photo by Paul Wodehouse

What does the mayor of Honolulu do when he's in Edmonton? For Frank Fasi (second from left), the answer was simple – head to the water and the waves of West Edmonton Mall's World Waterpark. Fasi posed with Triple Five Corp. owner and managing director Nader Ghermezian and some bathing beauties at the waterpark's official opening.

Bitter And Brutal

It was one of the longest and most bitter labour disputes in the province's history.

It began June 1, 1986 when 1,080 members of United Food and Commercial Workers Local 280P walked out of the Gainers meat-packing plant demanding wage parity with employees at other Canadian packing plants.

One day after that happened a court injunction limited the number of people who could picket at the Peter Pocklington-owned north-side plant on 66 Street.

The next day all hell broke loose as hundreds of unionized workers ignored the court order and used rocks, bottles and sticks to try to stop buses carrying replacement employees from entering the business.

About 200 city police officers were dispatched to the scene and arrested 115 strikers.

Tempers were red hot that day. Union workers were furious at the thought others were replacing them at their jobs.

"We don't want those people here and that's that," spat unionist Darrel MacKouey, who admitted flinging one of many rocks at the buses.

"Sure I threw a rock and I'll throw other ones," he said. "We're not going to stand for this BS. We're mad as hell and we've got nothing to lose."

All of it was spurred when Pocklington refused to follow the lead of Canada Packers, which had granted its workers a wage hike of 51 cents an hour in the first year of a contract and 52 cents an hour in the second year.

The violence outside the plant continued for most of June, with mass arrests of defiant workers and a spate of criminal charges for those accused of the most violent incidents.

Sun photo by Gary Bartlet

Cops remove a striker from in front of the Gainers packing plant during the long strike. City police spent $500,000 in overtime in June 1986 alone, trying to keep the peace during the strike.

Sun file photo

ABOVE: Angry pickets threw eggs and garbage at the front of a bus trying to take non-union workers into the Gainers plant during the strike.
BELOW: An Edmonton police officer standing on the front of another bus, this one with the windshield almost completely ripped off the front, tried to stop angry union members from attacking it.

City police said they spent $500,000 for overtime in June alone, trying to keep the peace while allowing replacement workers to safely enter the aging plant.

By mid-August more than 460 people had been arrested – and there was no end in sight for the bitter dispute.

There were brief hopes for a resolution when Pocklington and union officials met for the first time Sept. 4. But talks broke down the next day when the sides could not agree over replacement workers keeping jobs after the strike.

At the end of September Pocklington added fuel to the fire, saying business at his replacement-worker-run plant was so good he didn't care if the dispute was ever settled.

There was a break in the ugly dispute Oct. 28 when the Alberta Labour Relations Board ruled Gainers bargained unfairly at the beginning of the strike.

It also ruled in favour of the union on its charges of unfair labour practices and unfair cancellation of the workers' pension plan.

On Nov. 21 the labour board ordered Gainers to give the union a complete contract offer within 10 days.

But that was still not the break needed to end the strike since the Gainers offer guaranteed replacement workers jobs before strikers, something that infuriated the union members.

In early December, Premier Don Getty applied pressure. A few days after that a provincial mediator joined the contract talks and a memorandum of agreement was finally hammered out Dec.11.

The workers voted to approve the pact that guaranteed they would be rehired ahead of non-union workers.

Still, their battle for wage parity had failed. There was no wage increase in the contract for 1987 or 1988.

Sun photo by Gary Bartlett

Principal Group Collapse

It took 14 long years to conclude one of Alberta's worst financial collapses.

In 2001, investors in Principal Group got their final payment after a long struggle.

The Edmonton-based company collapsed in 1987, taking thousands of people's investments in the process.

Back in 2001 investors got to split up the final proceeds of the company – carving up $7.8 million from the sale of the Cormie Ranch west of Edmonton.

Former Principal Group founder Don Cormie, many of his relatives, partner Ken Marlin and Christa Petracca were the prime defendants in what was the final part of the Principal Group saga – a class-action lawsuit.

"It took a hell of a long time but it's better than a kick in the butt," said Ken Pennifold, spokesman for the Principal Investors Protection Society.

The Principal companies, First Investors and Associated Investors, were forced into receivership in 1987.

That left about 60,000 investors in six provinces out nearly $500 million. Many of them were seniors who had invested their life savings.

A lengthy inquiry by Calgary lawyer Bill Code later found evidence tending to show fraud and dishonesty in the companies' operations.

As well, the Alberta government was roasted for not doing an adequate job of monitoring the financial companies.

The inquiry went on for 205 days.

It heard from more than 150 witnesses.

None of the defendants were criminally charged.

However, in 1992, Don Cormie pleaded guilty under the Investors Act to misleading investors and was fined $500,000.

Investors recouped some of their money from the government and also slowly got cash back from the companies' receivers.

It took investors about three years to get most of their cash back.

The rest of the money came trickling back from the sale of company assets.

After the saga concluded it was estimated Alberta investors got back about 90% of their money – slightly more than people in other provinces where governments put in less reimbursement cash.

Sun photo by Robert Tayl

Like hundreds of others, Nancy Tchir, 70, faced a security guard and locked doors when she tried to recover the $1,000 she and her husband John had deposited in the downtown offices of Principal Savings and Trust. 'We wanted it to pay for our funerals,' she said.

CHAPTER SIX

City of Champions

Edmonton has earned its title City of Champions.

Not only are we a progressive metropolis of nearly one million people, we have hosted some of the most prestigious sporting events on the planet, not the least of which was the 1978 Commonwealth Games and the 2001 World Championships in Athletics.

Along the way our professional sports teams have scooped numerous titles. From the Oilers' five Stanley Cups to the Eskimos' five Grey Cups in a row, our local sports heroes have done us proud.

...un photographer Christine Vanzella won the Canadian Press Sports Picture of the Month award for June 2002 with this photo of the ...5-kilogram Greco-Roman class competition at the 5th World University Wrestling Championships, held at the University of Alberta.

Sun photo by Perry Mah

Wayne Gretzky wipes away a tear at a news conference after a ceremony Oct. 1, 1999, retiring his jersey, No. 99, from his days with the Edmonton Oilers. The ceremony was held at Skyreach Centre.

The Great One

It all began when a skinny, 17-year-old, 155-pound teenager stepped off a private jet in Edmonton.

The year was 1978 and Wayne Gretzky had just been traded to the Edmonton Oilers of the World Hockey Association from the Indianapolis Racers.

In the years to come, that skinny kid would rewrite NHL record books, put Edmonton on the map and be immortalized in the city that loved him.

The hockey phenomenon from Brantford, Ont., quickly lived up to his advance billing, winning rookie of the year for the WHA Oilers by scoring 110 points.

The next year – 1979 – was a bigger test for the gawky-looking centre iceman.

It was the year the Oilers and three other former WHA teams entered the NHL. Naysayers suggested Gretzky might have a tougher go of it in the more hard-hitting NHL.

It didn't turn out that way.

Gretzky not only survived the NHL, he turned the league on its ear.

Perhaps it was because he faithfully followed his father's basic tactic in tackling the game.

Walter Gretzky had long told his son: "Don't go where the puck was, go where the puck is going to be."

The junior Gretzky obviously took that to heart.

Before he retired about 20 years later, he held or shared an astounding 61 league records.

He scored 51 goals in that first 1979-80 season and 55 goals in the next one.

He won the Hart Trophy as the league's most valuable player that very first year and followed up the win by scooping the same honour seven years in a row.

Gretzky was just getting warmed up.

It took him just a few months in 1981-82 to shatter what was arguably the most impressive record in hockey – 50 goals in 50 games.

That mark had first been set by the legendary Montreal Canadien Maurice "The Rocket" Richard, in 1944-45.

Gretzky obliterated the record in amazing fashion on Dec.

30, 1982. That was the night The Great One scored five goals in a home game against Philadelphia.

That head-spinning feat gave Gretzky 50 goals in just 39 games – a mark hockey pundits feel may never be equalled.

In the same season, Gretzky pummelled some other long-time records.

The most impressive was his shattering of Phil Esposito's record for most goals in a season – 76.

Gretzky finished the season with 92 goals. Along the way he also managed to eclipse Esposito's other single-season

Sun photo by Perry Mah

LEFT: As the statue commemorating his years as an Edmonton Oiler looms in the background, Wayne Gretzky thanks Edmontonians for honouring him. He was taking part in an unveiling ceremony Aug. 28, 1989, for the statue, which is on permanent display in front of what is now known as Skyreach Centre. ABOVE: Sculptor John Weaver appears to be holding up the 6,000-kg statue as he oversees its installation in this Nov. 29, 1989 photo. The artwork was held aloft by a crane.

Sun photo by Paul Wodehouse

87

Sun photos by Perry Mah

Wayne Gretzky and friend Joey Moss hold up the Gretzky banner before it is raised to the rafters during a special ceremony at Skyreach Centre Oct. 1, 1999, to retire his number.

record of 152 points. Gretz buried that by notching 212 points.

Despite being surrounded by some of the best talent ever assembled on one team, it took Gretzky and Co. a bit longer to realize the dream of winning a Stanley Cup.

They did it May 19, 1984 by sweeping the powerful New York Islanders in four games straight.

Before his career with the Oilers ended Gretzky would lead the team to three more Cup victories.

During those years Gretzky set records that may never be beaten, including:
- 139 two-goal games
- 246 three-point games
- 14 five-assist games
- 123 four-point games
- 67 five-point games
- 20 six-point games
- Seven seven-point games.

There was universal praise for his talent throughout his

Gretzky waves to the crowd gathered at the Oilers Reunion '99 event at Northlands AgriCom Aug. 25, 1999, after being presented with his jersey as an Oilers alumnus.

career from virtually all opponents.

Superstar Mario Lemieux was among those who were most lavish in praise of Gretzky.

The day Gretzky retired, on April 18, 1999, Lemieux heaped praise on The Great One.

"He changed the game when he came into the league in the '80s," said the man they call Super Mario.

"The game really changed when he came along.

"Offensively, he did things nobody's ever going to be able to do. Just the way he was able to turn on a dime like nobody else can, his vision, his anticipation of the play, his passing....

"There's never been a passer in the past and there won't be one in the future who is going to be able to pass the puck flat all the time.

"And I think I can say his records are pretty safe."

When asked whether sniper Jaromir Jagr would take over from Gretzky after No. 99's retirement, Lemieux scoffed.

"Jagr's Jagr. Gretzky, like I said, is the greatest of all time. There's never going to be another Gretzky."

Sun file photo

Wayne Gretzky blows out the candles on a miniature hockey stick as he celebrates his 18th birthday in this Jan. 24, 1979 photo.

The 1978 Commonwealth Games

Edmonton showed the planet it could put on world-class sporting events – and the city did just that, hosting the XI Commonwealth Games in August 1978.

After a brutal showing medal-wise at the 1976 Montreal Summer Olympics, Canadian athletes kicked butt at Edmonton's Games that saw 47 countries compete.

Canada wound up at the top of the medal heap with 109, including 45 gold, 31 silver and 33 bronze.

England came second overall with 88 medals while Australia scooped 84.

It was the first and only time Canada had won the most medals at the Commonwealth Games and the team did it impressively.

The nation bested the powerful Australians in swimming, winning 15 gold medals compared with 10 for the Aussies.

The sweetest part of that was Edmonton's Graham Smith, who won a whopping six of those glittering medals.

Canada also had a hammerlock on wrestling success. It swept that sport, winning six gold and three silver medals.

Our nation took all four golds available in gymnastics, four of six in shooting and two of four in diving.

It was mainly smooth sailing on other fronts as well.

It was a virtual sellout of tickets and included a visit by Queen Elizabeth and various heads of state.

The weather was sunny and warm.

The biggest cloud on the horizon came when the powerful Nigerian team pulled out of the Games

Sun file photo

Seated on the steps, high up in Commonwealth Stadium, a youngster gets an uninterrupted view of the opening ceremonies.

Sun photo by Sean Young

ABOVE: Veteran Ottawa distance star Penny Werthner, left, passed tiring Anne Mackie-Morelli one step before the finish of the 800 metres but had to wait out an appeal to make it official when electronic timers recorded it the other way around.

RIGHT: Kenyan boxer Douglas Maina is a victim of a devastating knockout punch from his opponent, Tumat Sogolik of Papua New Guinea.

– Sun file photo

before the start.

Nigerian politicians attributed the boycott to the fact New Zealand was sending a team to the Games and that country maintained sports relations with South Africa, a nation despised by Nigeria.

The pullout was roundly criticized by athletes and politicians.

The comments of an Australian wrestling manager were typical of many.

Said Geoff Jameson: "I am here for sport. We are all here for sport. It should be sport first. Sport is sport and if that's their attitude, it isn't sporting."

It was feared scores of other African nations would follow the Nigerian boycott by pulling out, but that didn't happen.

Sun file photo

There must be an easier way to earn a medal. Aussie wrestler Ken Hoyt must be thinking along those lines under the weight of Canada's Raymond Takahashi. Takahashi won.

RIGHT: Joe Sax, No. 131, holds off a challenge by Albertan Rob Evans in the 3,000-metre steeplechase at Commonwealth Stadium.

INSET: This group of dancers from Sri Lanka were part of a broad range of international performers at Festival 78, held in conjunction with the Commonwealth Games.

Sun photo by Tom Walker

Sun file photo

Edmonton Eskimos

The Edmonton Eskimos have had a proud history of being the flagship franchise of the Canadian Football League.

But it was the club's dominance from 1978 to 1982 that was truly head-spinning.

Those were the years the Eskimos reeled off five Grey Cup victories in a row, led by legendary quarterback Warren Moon.

The team began that streak by beating the Montreal Alouettes 20-13 in the 1978 Cup game.

In 1979 Moon was hitting his stride and led the Esks to a 44-14 Grey Cup victory over the home-town Alouettes.

After the thrashing Edmonton's star quarterback was typically gracious, telling reporters, "Montreal makes you prepare better than most teams. And this week we were prepared."

The following year the Edmonton dynasty took out its frustrations during the Grey Cup game on the Hamilton Tiger-Cats, clawing them 48-10.

The Esks dream team had to battle back hard in the 1981 Grey Cup game, despite entering the game as heavy favourites after finishing the season with 14 wins, one tie and one loss.

The five-win, 11-loss Ottawa Rough Riders came within a whisker of stopping the Esks' Grey Cup streak but lost the game 26-23.

The Green and Gold capped their incredible Grey Cup streak by defeating the Toronto

Sun file photo

Beginning in 1979, Brian Kelly, seen catching the ball in this September 1979 photo, was an integral part of the Eskimos' march to five consecutive Grey Cups.

Sun file photos

ABOVE: Warren Moon, No. 1, seen here trying to outrun the Winnipeg defence in this August 1982 photo, quarterbacked the Eskimos to five consecutive Grey Cups from 1978 to 1982.

RIGHT: In a lighter moment, a group of Eskimos posed in 1980 for the Edmonton-based makers of Alberta Crude jeans. Moonlighting as models are, from left, Ed Jones, Angelo Santucci, Dale Potter, Dan Kepley, Pete Lavorato, Ron Estay and Tom Towns.

Argonauts in the 1982 championship by a score of 32-16.

It would be a few years before the team would get a sniff of victory again.

It took the local gridiron heroes five years to get back into the winner's circle.

In 1987 the Esks squeaked out a 38-36 Grey Cup game win over the Toronto Argonauts at B.C. Place in Vancouver.

Six years later the Esks won their next – and most recent – Cup, bouncing Winnipeg 33-23.

Our city first actually hosted the Grey Cup game in 1984 and again in 1997 – but the Esks faltered and did not make it to those Cup finals.

In 2002 the city once again hosted the Cup – and the home team did get to play, but lost 25-16 to the Montreal Alouettes in front of 62,531 fans at Commonwealth Stadium.

Pundits noted the Esks didn't lose the game so much as beat themselves through a series of dropped passes and untimely fumbles.

The Esks lost despite having a 25-7 edge in first downs over the Alouettes and a 417-300 advantage in total offence.

After that last Grey Cup appearance Eskimos quarterback Ricky Ray summed up the thoughts of many.

"It wasn't like we went out and played our best game and lost," said Ray. "It could have been so much different."

Sun file phot

LEFT: Eskimo Leo Blanchard reacts after the Eskimos beat the Argos in B.C. Place to win the 1987 Grey Cup. It marked the club's fourth championship of the decade.
ABOVE: The Eskimos bench reacts just moments before Jerry Kauric's Grey Cup-winning field goal in B.C. Place.

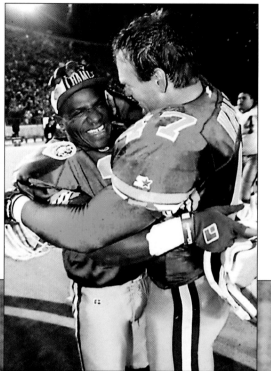

LEFT: Eskimos running back Gizmo Williams celebrates after Edmonton's Grey Cup win over the Winnipeg Blue Bombers in Calgary.
BELOW: The Eskimos squad hoists the Grey Cup for a celebratory group photo after the victory. That year, 1993, is the most recent Grey Cup win for the Edmonton Eskimos.

Sun photos by Perry Mah

Gorm Larsen captured this March 12, 1996 image of runner Eric Jobin collapsing after completing the men's 3,000-metre race at an indoor track event held at the University of Alberta's Butterdome. The photo won a Sun Media Dunlop Award for Sports Photography.

Sun photo by Gary Bartlett

The Canadian team marches into Commonwealth Stadium during the opening ceremonies of Universiade. Edmonton was the first Canadian city to host the games, which attracted 4,500 athletes from 85 countries.

1983 World University Games

Five years after holding the Commonwealth Games in 1978, our city played host to the world again.

The occasion was the less-well-known world university games or Universiade, held here in 1983 with 4,500 athletes from 85 countries.

On the scoreboard Canada did well enough, placing third with 38 medals, behind the Soviet Union with 115, and the United States with 55.

Most of the memories attached to those games were not strictly surrounding the medal performances.

One of the highlights for many was the fact Prince Charles and Lady Di were here at Commonwealth Stadium to kick off the event July 1, 1983.

The prince quickly won over the crowd when he told them, "It is the birthday of my dear wife. She had the good sense and excellent taste to be born on Canada's national day, which we celebrate today, the 116th anniversary of Confederation."

Others were wowed by memories of the opening ceremonies, which included 3,600 dancers, four-storey-high

Sun photo by Gary Bartle

Athletes hold torches high during the opening ceremonies of the world university games at Commonwealth Stadium.

inflatable animals, a giant map and an aerial display by Canada's Snowbirds.

Many will recall the wackier stories from those games, including a Canadian athlete taking a bathroom break in the middle of his track and field event.

Quebecer Guillaume Leblanc felt the call of nature, so he stopped at a washroom in the middle of his 20-km walk.

Despite the pit stop he won the event.

Fencer Jean-Marie Banos made headlines during the games for all the wrong reasons.

He became angry and kicked his fencing mask, hitting Italian fencing judge Stefano Pantono right in his family jewels.

Despite the fun and games, Universiade was marred by

**LEFT: Canada's Marie Louise Leblanc and Hua Hua Li of China compete in women's fencing.
BELOW: Men's gymnastics.**

Sun file photo

Sun photo by Robert Taylor

– Sun file photo

Members of the Canadian men's basketball squad celebrate during competition at the games. It turns out they had plenty to celebrate. Canada stunned the basketball community when it defeated the U.S. team, which included future NBA stars like Charles Barkley and Karl Malone, by a score of 85-77 to advance to the gold-medal match. Canada took the gold with an 83-68 victory over Yugoslavia. The U.S. took bronze, beating Cuba 199-91.

an unforgettable and horrifying tragedy.

The Soviet Union's Sergei Chalibashwili smashed the back of his skull against the 10-metre diving platform at Kinsmen Aquatic Centre in front of more than 800 spectators.

Chalibashwili was in the second revolution of an extremely difficult dive – a reverse 3½ somersault – when the accident happened.

The crowd gasped at the sound of the accident and looked on in horror as the diver fell into the pool, blood pouring from his ears and mouth.

Other divers cringed at the accident, including Canadian David Snively.

"I've seen divers break their feet when they've hit the diving board, but this is the worst thing I have ever seen," said Snively.

Chalibashwili died in hospital about one week later.

RIGHT: Team Canada cheers a victory in men's volleyball during the games.
BELOW: Swimming action at the games.

Sun photo by Paul Wodehouse

Sun file photo

Sun photo by Robert Taylor

ABOVE: Premier Peter Lougheed and Princess Diana chat during the opening ceremonies of Universiade, July 1, 1983.
RIGHT: Spectators celebrate during Universiade's closing ceremonies July 11.

Sun file photo

First And Sweetest

The talent-rich Edmonton Oilers teams of the 1980s and early 1990s were a true dynasty, winning five Stanley Cups.

But most fans and pundits agree the first Cup win was the sweetest.

In May 1984, just five years after entering the National Hockey League, the Oilers won hockey's holy grail by beating the New York Islanders four games to one.

The Oilers were loaded with young stars including Wayne Gretzky, Mark Messier, Glenn Anderson, Jari Kurri, Paul Coffey and Grant Fuhr, among others.

Messier that year won the Conn Smythe Trophy as the most valuable player of the playoffs. He had scored 26 points in the post-season.

Naturally the 23-year-old was most ecstatic about winning that other trophy – the Stanley Cup.

After skating around the ice clutching the Cup while carrying it over his head, a grinning Messier gushed, "I'd been rehearsing that moment for five years. I've been dreaming about skating around with it since I was six years old."

The road to the Cup began against the Winnipeg Jets, a team the Oilers swept in a best-of-five series.

Jari Kurri starred in the first game of the series, scoring a hat trick as his team drubbed the Jets 9-2. The Oilers had built up a 5-1 lead in the first period.

It took a goal in overtime from Randy Gregg to beat the Jets in the second game of the series.

The Oilers swept the Jets by winning 4-1 in the third game of the best-of-five series.

The arch-rival Calgary Flames turned out to be the Oilers' toughest opponent on the road to Lord Stanley's magnificent mug.

The Oilers had the Flames on the mat with a 3-1 series lead but the Cowtown crew came back to force a seventh game.

That deciding game had fans holding their breath. The

Sun photo by Paul Wodehouse

This accidental double exposure photo shows Wayne Gretzky celebrating and, later on, Mark Messier taking a drink from the Stanley Cup.

home team trailed 4-3 when Flame Al MacInnis notched a goal at 10:15 of the second period.

But the Oilers players responded the way they did a lot in those days. The team scored four straight goals to dispatch the Flames to the golf course.

The Minnesota North Stars did not fare as well as the Flames against the Oilers.

The very first game of the Campbell Conference final, the Stars were blown out 7-1.

Gretzky scored the winner in Game 2 as the Oilers beat the Stars 4-3.

Game 3 saw Dave Lumley take what seemed to be a costly major penalty. The Stars scored three goals on the resulting power play to take a 5-2 lead.

The Oilers barely flinched and responded with six goals in a row to win 8-5.

Edmonton finished off the Stars in Bloomington, Minnesota, winning 3-1 to advance to the Stanley Cup final against the Islanders.

The 1984 Cup win was followed by other Cup victories – a 4-1 series win in the 1985 Stanley Cup final against Philadelphia, a 4-3 series victory in 1987 over Philly, a 4-0 game sweep versus Boston in 1988 and a 4-1 win in 1990 against those same Beantown Bruins.

While sports pundits had picked the Oilers to win the Cup in 1984, most did not think the team could knock off a squad as powerful as the Islanders in five games by some convincing scores.

Sun file photo
Kevin Lowe, left, and Paul Coffey after the victory.

105

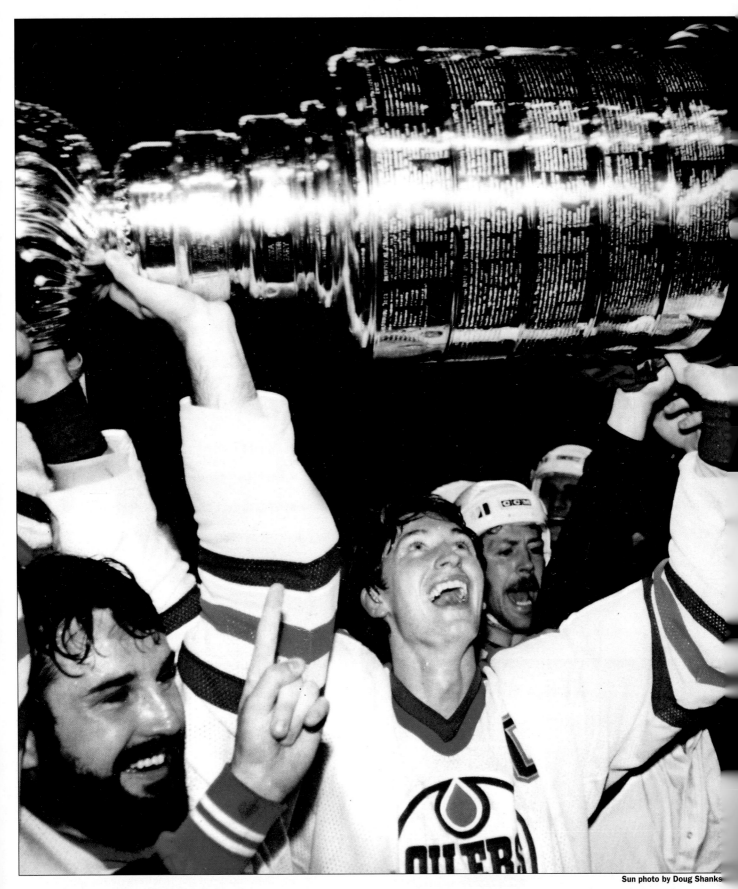

Sun photo by Doug Shanks

Disbelief on the part of the Oilers could be excused, as the players probably didn't expect that they would not only beat the Islanders, but rout the defending Stanley Cup champs, taking the final series in five games.

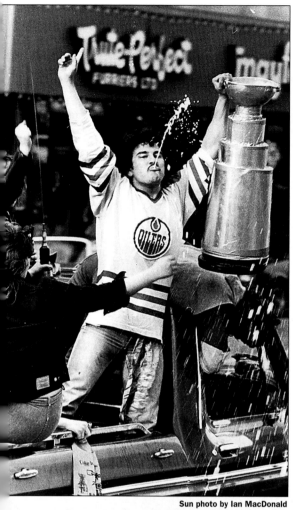

Over the series, the Oilers outscored the mighty Islanders 19-6.

Said *Hockey News* editor Bob McKenzie: "It's a little shocking. And I don't mean that as a knock on the Oilers. I think if you asked the Oilers if they'd win this series in five and not just by beating (the Islanders) but routing them, they'd tell you they're a little shocked themselves."

While the vast majority of Edmontonians reacted to the win with high-fives and heartfelt happiness, hundreds of others in the downtown area ran amok and had to be quelled by riot police.

The ugly incidents came hours after a civic parade was held to celebrate the win, with more than 100,000 fans lining the streets.

Later, roughly 2,000 fans – scores of whom were drunk – taunted 75 police officers on Jasper Avenue near 101 Street by tossing rocks and beer bottles at them.

Riot police responded by swinging billy clubs and arresting 65 of the rowdiest Cup crazies.

Police information officer Const. Ian MacKechnie was disgusted by the behaviour of the rowdies.

"These people aren't Oilers fans," he hissed. "They're just trouble-makers taking advantage of the whole situation."

The riot occurred when a crowd was hosed down by firefighters after the fans were told by police to disperse, but didn't.

LEFT: After the victory parade downtown the scene turned ugly as about 2,000 people, many of them drunk, became rowdy and refused to disperse.
BELOW: Riot police responded by bringing out the dogs, swinging billy clubs and arresting 65 of the worst offenders.

Sun photo by Ian MacDonald

Sun photo by Robert Taylor

Gorm Larsen won a Sun Media Dunlop Award for this July 31, 1990 sports picture. It was taken right after George Foreman had delivered his knockout punch to Canadian champ Ken Lakusta in a fight held at the AgriCom.

The Wedding, Then *The* Trade

It was dubbed The Royal Wedding – and few events in Edmonton's history attracted the attention of Edmontonians as did Wayne Gretzky's nuptials on July 16,1988.

Wayne chose Edmonton's St. Joseph's Basilica to tie the knot with Hollywood actress Janet Jones, as thousands of ordinary Edmontonians gathered outside to catch a glimpse of the couple.

Janet wore a $40,000 satin gown and $250,000 worth of jewelry, including a sizable wedding ring. The guest list was a who's who of hockey, sprinkled with Hollywood celebrities such as Alan Thicke, David Foster and Tim Feehan.

Wayne's best man was longtime pal Eddie Mio. His groomsmen included Mark Messier, Kevin Lowe, Paul Coffey and his brothers Glen, Brent and Keith.

The Great One walked down the aisle at the side of his parents, Walter and Phyllis Gretzky.

The superstar was slightly nervous looking during the ceremony but looked relieved when the pair left the church.

The 3,000 or so people gathered outside cheered when the couple posed for them on the steps of the church and kissed.

It looked as if Wayne and Janet would become Edmonton's unofficial royal couple and live happily ever after in the city that worshipped them.

Sun photo by Peter Cutler

Wayne and Janet depart from St. Joseph's Basilica following their July 16, 1988 wedding ceremony.

Sun file photo

The newlywed couple kiss after the ceremony. Their happiness was disrupted less than a month later when Oilers' owner Peter Pocklington announced Gretzky's trade to the Los Angeles Kings Aug. 9, 1988.

But it was not to be.

Rumours of the unthinkable began to swirl only a couple of weeks after the wedding. On Aug. 4, 1988 a *Sun* columnist revealed storm clouds on the horizon: "The rumour has been running rampant for days: Wayne Gretzky to the Los Angeles Kings for $18 million."

It was quickly followed by denials from management and Oilers' owner Peter Pocklington. Oilers president Glen Sather staunchly denied there was any trade in the works.

"There is nothing to it," he said.

"Every summer there's a different rumour. This one goes in the same bin as all the other ones.

"If there was anything like that, I assume Peter Pocklington would let me know. There's nothing to it."

Pocklington angrily denied the rumours as late as a day before the sale and trade of Gretzky, Aug. 9, 1988.

The deal saw the Oilers trade centres Gretzky and Mike Krushelnyski and defenceman Marty McSorley to the L.A. Kings for forwards Jimmy Carson and Martin Gelinas, first-round draft picks in 1989, 1991 and 1993, and $18 million.

110

Initially the anger of fans and media turned on Janet. Many critics surmised the Hollywood starlet demanded her man be traded to Los Angeles.

She later set the record straight.

"Peter Pocklington is the reason Wayne Gretzky is no longer an Edmonton Oiler," she told *The Sun*.

She said the whole thing was put in motion when, five days after their wedding, "Pocklington gave Kings' owner Bruce McNall permission to take Wayne if he could do it."

Pocklington had long stuck to the story that it was Gretzky who wanted the trade, something vehemently denied by Janet.

"The story of the trade as presented by Peter Pocklington is false. Pocklington is the reason Wayne is gone," she said.

"The day after the Stanley Cup, Pocklington told Wayne about an offer from Vancouver. Wayne said to Pocklington: 'I can't believe you coming to me with this the day after we win the Stanley Cup.'"

Sun photo by Paul Wodehouse

ABOVE: Janet Gretzky addresses the media at the Aug. 10, 1988 press conference held to introduce Wayne as a Los Angeles King. She later told *The Sun* the trade was Pocklington's idea, and that the newlywed couple had been prepared to spend the rest of their lives in Edmonton.

Sun photo by Peter Cutler

. visibly agitated Gretzky sits next to a visibly uncomfortable Pocklington during the press conference to announce the trade.

Pocklington later backed out of that deal.

"Before the wedding, Wayne had heard so many rumours about being traded and sold he asked Pocklington about them. Pocklington suggested Wayne come to his office to talk about it. He told Wayne there was nothing to them."

"This was the day before our wedding. I brought my car to Edmonton. We had every intention of living the rest of our lives in Edmonton."

Ten years after the trade, Sather offered his blow-by-blow account of precisely what happened, beginning on the very day of the news conference to announce the trade.

"I took Wayne into a room with just the two of us at Molson House where we held the press conference," said Sather.

"I told him I'd stop the deal. I told him I'd tell Peter I'd resign if he didn't stop the deal. But Wayne decided not to because he felt it was all beyond repair at that point."

Sather said he was the last to know about the deal that was secretly struck by Puck.

"Peter invited me to President Ford's golf tournament in Beaver Creek, Colorado.

"That's when he told me. I got on the phone to Bruce McNall from there. That's when I began to understand that the deal was already done.

"Peter was afraid to tell me and I don't blame him."

Gretzky reflected back on that dreaded day, when he broke down and cried at the news conference announcing his trade.

"It's the hardest thing I've ever been through," he said.

"I think about it a lot still. I don't think there's an Aug. 9 that's gone by when I haven't thought about it.

"At the time we were the cream of the crop. We'd just won our fourth Stanley Cup.

"I played as well as I ever played in that final. Then all of a sudden, things happen. And, unfortunately, it all ended a little too quick."

Sun photo by Perry Ma

There were few dry eyes at the Aug. 9, 1988 press conference, least of all Gretzky's.

CHAPTER SEVEN
TJ's
Top 25

Sun photo by Perry Mah

Stalwart Edmonton Sun sports personality Terry Jones has covered the past 25 years of sports in Edmonton and shares some of the highlights here.

When they asked me, for the purposes of this publication and the celebration of the 25th anniversary of *The Sun*, to list the 25 greatest moments in Edmonton sport, I didn't have to think about it for more than a second.

"No chance," I said. "Can't be done. Any other town, no problem. Not here. Not this city. Not this paper."

Think about it, they said.

Over the span of a few months, I thought about it a lot. I started keeping a list, to prove my point. The list kept getting longer and longer as I thought of this event and that moment, this championship and that memory.

The exercise reinforced what I already knew. We've been spoiled in this city. And more than anybody, I've been blessed to be the one sportswriter, the one media member who was privileged to touch each and every story over that span.

There are papers with 125 years of history that haven't had the sports stories, the events, the moments we've experienced in Edmonton and that I've covered here.

Wayne Gretzky alone had 46 records while in an Edmonton Oilers uniform, any one of which would make this list in most cities.

Three Grey Cup championships and six Brier wins didn't make my list.

Neither did Ron Kittle's 50-home-run year for the Edmonton Trappers in 1982. Nor did the Trappers' four Pacific Coast League championships.

The University of Alberta Bears and Pandas with their dozens of titles. Not on the list.

Edmonton played a large part in the success of the 1988 Olympic Winter Games in Calgary where the wife of Oilers GM Kevin Lowe, Edmonton-born Karen Percy, won two bronze medals. Not on the list.

Kristi Yamaguchi, skating out of Edmonton's Royal Glenora Club, won world championships and an Olympic gold medal for the U.S. Didn't make the list.

Willie de Wit won an Olympic silver medal and fought Ken Lakusta of Edmonton in front of the largest boxing crowd of the year. Becky Scott, Edi Podovinsky, Jeremy

Sun photo by Paul Wodehouse

Edmonton Trapper Ron Kittle is struck by a pitch from Portland's Mercedes Esquer as he tries for his 50th home run of the year in this Aug. 31, 1982 photo. Kittle achieved that lofty goal but his achievement didn't make Terry Jones's list of the 25 greatest moments in Edmonton sport over the past 25 years; neither did the Trappers' four Pacific Coast League championships.

Wotherspoon, David Ford, Tim Berrett, Jennifer Heil, Deidra Dionne … the list is so long I'm offending more athletes than I'm honouring just by including this paragraph of those relatively recent headliners.

The NHL All-Star Game and the NHL draft were held here. There were the great moments of all the Canadian Finals Rodeos and Canadian Derbies.

Remember Kai Haaskivi, the world's greatest indoor soccer player, and Timo Liekoski's Edmonton Drillers team, which won the North American Soccer League indoor title before 16,257 fans in Chicago Stadium? How about Arnold Palmer, who, after five years without a win, finally won another golf tournament, beating Gary Player and others in the Labatt International at the Mayfair in 1980? What about home-town hero Perry Lychak's pitching performance in a 2-1 win over Cuba in one of the two intercontinental cups we held here? What about the 1990 World Baseball Championships? The 1980 World Amateur Wrestling Championships? The 1992 World Water-ski Championships? The 1999 World Taekwondo Championships? The 2001 World Triathlon Championships?

And what about the last game Brazil played before going south and winning the '94 World Cup of soccer – the one which drew 54,000 and recorded the first million-dollar gate in Canadian soccer history? How about Davis Cup tennis and LPGA golf ...?

There are events we've *forgotten* that other writers with other papers in other cities would put on their list.

And what about the Salt Lake City 2002 Olympic Winter Games hockey gold medal? From ex-Oilers Wayne Gretzky and Kevin Lowe running the show to ex-Oil King Pat Quinn and ex-Edmontonian Ken Hitchcock on the coaching staff, to Oilers Ryan Smyth and Eric Brewer on the team and the Oilers support staff of Barrie Stafford, Ken Lowe, Stew Poirier and Bill Tuele, it was a massive local story from start to finish. It finished with the team digging their lucky loonie, placed in the ice by Olympic ice-maker Trent Evans of Edmonton, out of the ice to take to the Hockey Hall of Fame. And as a backdrop to all of this were the 1952 Edmonton Mercurys, the last Canadian team to win an Olympic gold medal 50 years ago and made very much a part of it all. A month later and the Mercurys became the first team inducted into the Canadian Olympic Hall of Fame.

All of that, and so much more, didn't make it into my top 25.

Sun photo by Christine Vanzella

Members of the Edmonton Mercurys Olympic hockey team, from left, Jack Davies, Don Gauf, Bill Dawe, Monty Ford, Eric Paterson and Al Purvis pose with a picture of their 1952 team, the last Canadian squad to win Olympic gold in the 20th century. The team was inducted into the Hockey Hall of Fame a month after the 2002 Salt Lake City Winter Olympics – another moment that didn't make it into Jones's top 25.

Photo courtesy Alberta Report

1: 1978 Commonwealth Games

These highlights appear in chronological order, but the hosting of the Commonwealth Games, in one way, ranks No. 1 regardless. While we all still celebrate the six golds of Edmonton's Graham Smith in the pool and the gold medal on the track by Edmonton's Diane Jones-Konihowski and the only time Canada finished first in the medal count in the history of the Commonwealth Games, there was oh so much more involved. Hindsight proves that this was far more than a one-off hosting of the first return of these Games to Canada since Roger Bannister broke the four-minute mile in Vancouver in 1954. These were the biggest and best-organized Commonwealth Games ever held to that point. The sense of community and volunteerism that combined to fire a desire to play host to major international sports events and to make Edmonton one of the premier places on the planet for welcoming the world, began in 1978. In playing host to the Commonwealth Games, Edmonton found its identity.

Sun file photo

ABOVE: The opening of the Commonwealth Games Aug. 4, 1978 marked the beginning of the biggest and best-organized Commonwealth Games to that point and helped Edmonton find its identity.
TOP: Edmonton's own Graham Smith poses with his six gold medals.

Sun photo by Al Scott

LEFT: Canada's Desai Williams, Lane 2, beats his competitors across the finish line in the 100 metres.
ABOVE: Bruce Matheson of Canada keeps a close eye on the official as he checks to see which ball lies shot in the Games lawn bowling competition.

Sun file photo

Sun photo by Walter Tychnowicz

Former Eskimos quarterback Tom Wilkinson shows off his Grey Cup rings. After leading Edmonton to the league championship in 1975, Wilkinson remained with the squad until the end of the 1981 season, when the Eskimos took their fourth consecutive Cup.

2: Revenge For The Staples Game

It was known, for a few hours, as the 'Ice Bowl.' Forever after it would be legendary as 'The Staples Game.' It was the 1977 Grey Cup game in Montreal on a playing surface that was more skating rink than field. The Alouettes used a staple gun to give them traction that the Edmonton Eskimos couldn't find in a humiliating 41-6 loss. The team spent the entire year with only one thing in mind: Revenge. A 10-4-2 record and a 26-13 win over the Calgary Stampeders in the Western Final got them back to the Grey Cup against the Alouettes. And this time it was different. This time, with Tom Wilkinson the MVP of the game, the Eskimos won 20-13. It was a broken and busted Grey Cup that Wilkinson and Dan Kepley carried off the field that day, thanks to an RCMP horse on the field that caused Wilkinson to go one way and Kepley the other, with both keeping a firm grip on the Cup. But the Cup itself wasn't what it was about that year. "I couldn't have spent another winter in Edmonton if we'd lost," said Edmonton native Dave Fennell. "Everyone reminded us of 41-6 all winter long."

3: Three In A Row

Hugh Campbell said that the thing which amazed him the most about the Edmonton Eskimos team he coached in the late '70s and early '80s was how they managed to find a fresh goal every year. And how they managed to make themselves totally passionate about accomplishing their stated goal. And how they almost *willed* it to happen. The 1980 Grey Cup was easy. It was three in a row. Three makes it an official era in sport. And this was a group of guys who heard, over and over again, about the greatness of the 1954-55-56 Eskimos, the last team in the CFL to win three in a row. Winning the Grey Cup in 1980 meant these new Edmonton Eskimos had created their own place in history. In 1980 the Eskimos went 13-3 and scored 505 points. And they won the Grey Cup by the mind-boggling score of 48-10 over the Hamilton Tiger-Cats. It was the most lopsided win in modern-day Grey Cup history.

Sun file photo

Warren Moon, seen here dodging a Hamilton tackler during the Grey Cup game, was instrumental in leading the Eskimos to their third consecutive championship.

Sun file photo

ABOVE: Gretzky celebrates after scoring goal No. 46, his first of the night against the Flyers.
BELOW: A series of shots shows the reaction of Gretzky and a teammate after goal No. 50, scored on an empty net.

Sun photos by Paul Wodehouse

4: Gretzky: 50 In 39

It was 1944-45 and the Allied forces invaded France after storming the beaches of Normandy. Rocket Richard took people's minds off the Second World War when, on the 50th and final game of the season, he scored his 50th goal. After that it became the sexiest record in the sport. On Dec. 30, 1981, the Rocket's red glare became the flick of a Bic. The not-yet-turned-21-year-old who was already being called the greatest player in hockey history broke the greatest record in hockey with the latest, greatest game of his career. He scored five goals that night against the Philadelphia Flyers. Nine goals in two games. Fifty goals in 39 games. Goal No. 50 came into an empty net, with Pete Peeters, an Edmontonian who is now the Oilers goalie coach, out as an extra attacker. "What he did was absolutely amazing," said Peeters. But the few words Bobby Clarke said to Gretzky that night said it all: "I know everything that's been written about you. I think none of it is adequate."

5: Five In A Row

In 1981 the Eskimos came back from a shocking 41-6 deficit to win the game on the last play as, for the last time, Bob Howes snapped to Tom Wilkinson who put it down for Dave Cutler to kick it through the uprights to beat the Ottawa Rough Riders 26-23. It was Wilkinson's final game. A year later it was one last time for old times' sake. Hugh Campbell would leave for the USFL and then to the Houston Oilers of the NFL where he'd be joined by quarterback Warren Moon. This was a year in which Campbell would lock the dressing room door after a Labour Day loss in Calgary and a slow start to the season and ask the team for a commitment. He got it. The Eskimos dialled it up, finished with an 11-5 season and got back to the Grey Cup to go for five in a row and go out a dynasty. They'd leave Campbell with a .773 winning percentage, tops in all of CFL history, but barely. Pop Ivy's was .773 with the 1954-55-56 Eskimos. "I never saw a team so juiced up before a game," said Moon, who won Grey Cup MVP honours in the 36-16 win over the Toronto Argos, giving the Eskimos a win over every club in the Eastern Conference in their last four years of the five-year run.

Sun file photo

Eskimos coach Hugh Campbell took the team to its fifth Grey Cup in a row in 1982 before heading to the NFL and the Houston Oilers.

6: 1983 Universiade

The sun came out seconds before Prince Charles and Lady Di entered Commonwealth Stadium for the July 1 opening ceremonies. And Prince Charles melted the crowd with one line: "It's the birthday of my dear wife – she had the good sense and excellent taste to be born on Canada's national day." It was a terrific opening ceremonies with four-storey-high inflatable animals, 3,600 dancers and the Snowbirds. It was a games to be remembered for swimmer Alex Baumann and Jack Donohue's Canadian basketball team, which had their greatest moment upsetting the U.S., and the chilling moment when Russian diver Sergei Chalibashwili hit his head on the board and lost his life. But what the world would remember is that Edmonton did what international sports people said couldn't have been done anywhere else. Edmonton held two successful, major games in a span of five years.

Sun photo by Robert Taylor

Prince Charles, left, and Canadian Secretary of State Serge Joyal.

Sun file photo

Commonwealth Stadium was a riot of colour during the July 1, 1983 opening ceremonies for the world university games.

7: We Are The Champions

When Kevin Lowe announced his retirement, somebody asked him about his greatest thrill. "May 19, 1984," he said. Then the tears came. In a flood. "When Dave Lumley scored the empty-net goal. It was pretty unbelievable. When the puck went in the net. It will be forever in my mind." Indeed. The Edmonton Oilers – after scoring a record 446 goals in the regular season and going 57-18-5 – had won their first Stanley Cup. The pre-game sign on the dressing room wall said it all before the Oilers won Game 5 and the series against the four-in-a-row New York Islanders: "The Drive For Five is no longer alive because the thirst for first shall be quenched tonight." Edmonton went crazy. An estimated 200,000 people attended the biggest parade in city history. And thanks to a bet between mayors, 36 Long Island ducks were moving to Storyland Valley Zoo.

Sun file photo

Mark Messier with the Conn Smythe Trophy in the Stanley Cup victory parade in downtown Edmonton.

Sun photo by Paul Wodehouse

A jubilant Wayne Gretzky poses with his father, Walter, and brother Glen in the Oilers dressing room.

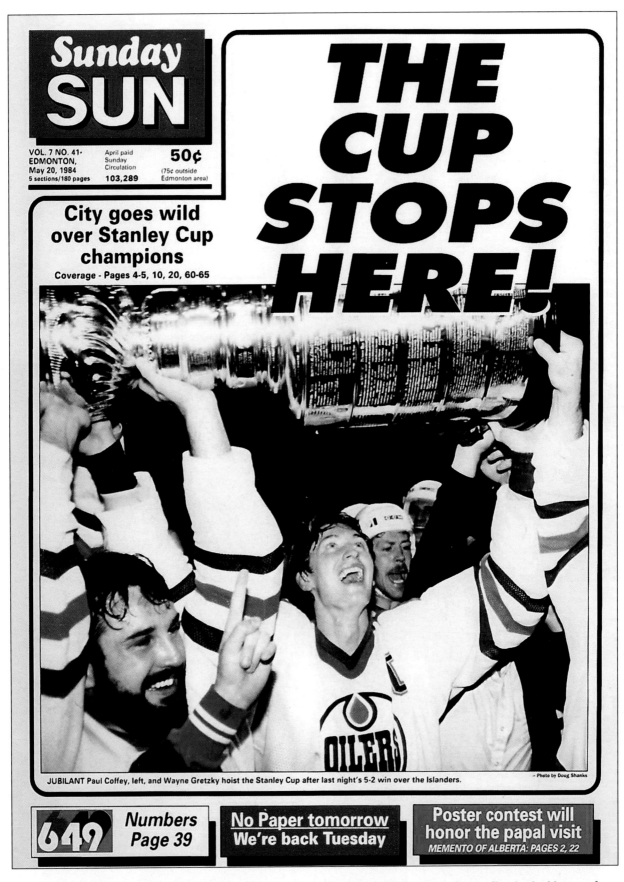

Sunday SUN

VOL. 7 NO. 41·
EDMONTON,
May 20, 1984
5 sections/180 pages

April paid
Sunday
Circulation

103,289

50¢

(75¢ outside
Edmonton area)

City goes wild over Stanley Cup champions

Coverage - Pages 4-5, 10, 20, 60-65

THE CUP STOPS HERE!

JUBILANT Paul Coffey, left, and Wayne Gretzky hoist the Stanley Cup after last night's 5-2 win over the Islanders.

– Photo by Doug Shanks

649 Numbers Page 39

No Paper tomorrow We're back Tuesday

Poster contest will honor the papal visit
MEMENTO OF ALBERTA: PAGES 2, 22

The May 20, 1984 front page of The Edmonton Sun trumpets the Oilers' Stanley Cup win, the first in the history of the young franchise.

8: The Cup Stays Here

The crowd chanted "The Cup Stays Here, The Cup Stays Here" throughout Game 5 as the Edmonton Oilers made it back-to-back Stanley Cups, this time against the Philadelphia Flyers. The Oilers – after starting their Cup defence by going undefeated in their first 15 games, en route to going 49-20-11 during the regular season – had won all 10 playoff games at home in front of the Northlands Coliseum crowd and, with their last six from the year before, broke the Montreal Canadiens' record for most consecutive home wins in the playoffs. For the stars of the squad it was two Stanley Cups and a Canada Cup within a span of 53 weeks. "We've got to be rated as good as any team that ever won two in a row," said Conn Smythe Trophy winner Wayne Gretzky as he drank from the Cup. "All I know is that 15 years from now, I'm going to say I played on a great hockey team."

Sun file photo

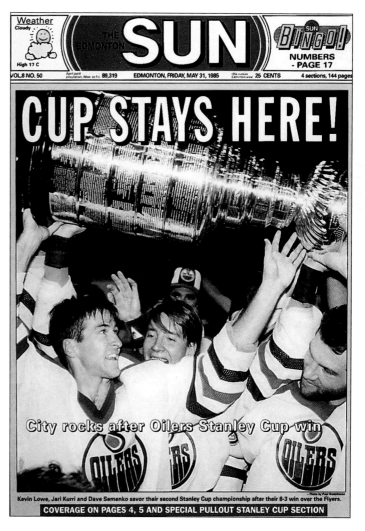

ABOVE: For the second year in a row, the front page of The Edmonton Sun, this time the May 31, 1985 edition, announces the Oilers victory in the Stanley Cup.
LEFT: A jubilant Mark Messier holds the Cup high as he skates around the Coliseum.

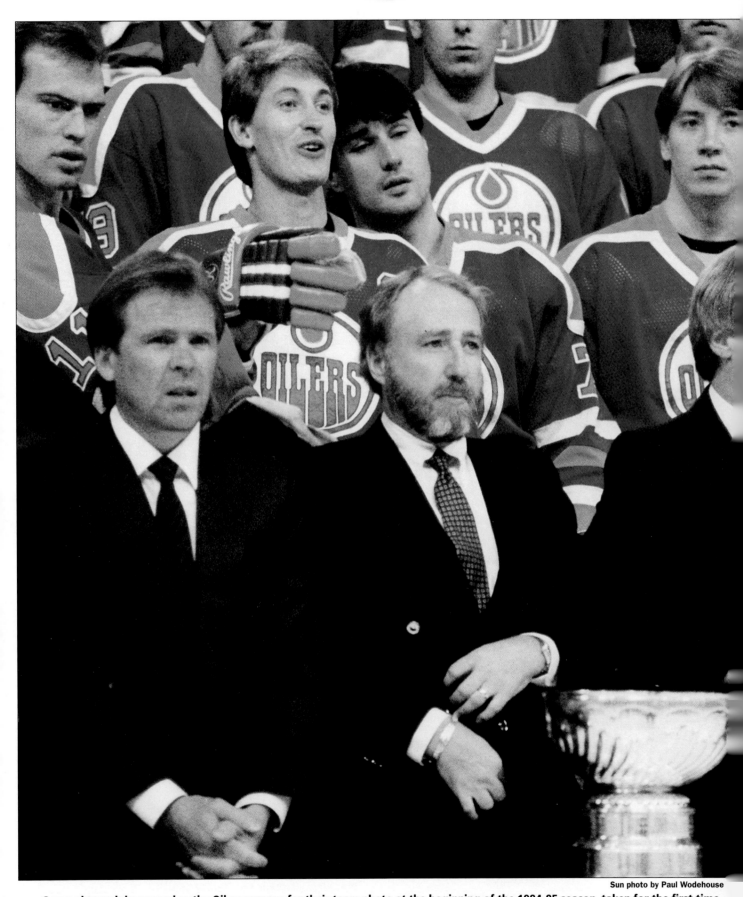

Sun photo by Paul Wodehouse

Some players joke around as the Oilers prepare for their team photo at the beginning of the 1984-85 season, taken for the first time with the Stanley Cup. By the end of the season they had ensured their next team photo would also feature Lord Stanley's trophy.

9: Still The One

On the back of a raw rookie on his 23rd birthday, a dynasty died. In the second round, against Calgary, Steve Smith scored on his own net to inspire the headline in *The Sun* the next morning: "Biggest Blunder Ever." A year later, in 1987, Edmonton was in a Game 7 again, except this time it was one of the few Game 7s in the history of the Stanley Cup final. Mark Messier, Jari Kurri and Glenn Anderson scored in a 3-1 win as the Oilers outshot the Flyers 43-20

and Philadelphia goalie Ron Hextall won the Conn Smythe Trophy. A year and a month after his 23rd birthday, Smith was crying again: "I was in tears last year and I'm in tears again this year. This time they're tears of joy." The freeze-frame moment came when Wayne Gretzky held the Stanley Cup over his head and then handed it over to Steve Smith to be the first to carry it. It would go down as one of the classiest acts in the history of sport.

Sun photo by Paul Wodehouse

Philadelphia netminder Ron Hextall was the centre of controversy after this chop against Edmonton's Kent Nilsson in the final series.

LEFT: As he hoists the Stanley Cup over his head, Wayne Gretzky's face reflects the joy felt by the rest of the Oilers, and much of Edmonton, when the city's NHL team won its second Cup in 1985.
BELOW: Wayne Gretzky handed the Cup to Steve Smith to carry first – one of the classiest acts in the history of sport.

Sun photo by Tom Braid

Sun file photo

10: Greatest Grey Cup Game Ever

It was, arguably, the greatest Grey Cup game ever played. And, at the time, there wasn't much argument. It will always be The Game for Brian Kelly and most of the Edmonton Eskimos who were in B.C. Place on Nov. 29, 1987 as the Eskimos won 38-36 over the Toronto Argos. "The last Grey Cup game I played will always be the one for me," said Kelly. "It was an incredible experience. It was the most exciting game in which I played in my entire career. It was a thrill to be in that." Henry "Gizmo" Williams scored a touchdown on a 115-yard missed field goal return and Jerry Kauric kicked a 49-yard field goal to win it in the final minute. A few months later and the Grey Cup and the Stanley Cup would sit together on the field at Commonwealth Stadium one sunny Sunday afternoon so that fans could have their pictures taken with both. And signs were being erected at every entrance to Edmonton: "City of Champions."

Sun photo by Doug Shanks

ABOVE: Eskimos tackles celebrate a take-down against the Argonauts during the 1987 Grey Cup game at B.C. Place. The Eskimos won 38-36. RIGHT: Eskies fans in a local bar celebrate the victory, arguably one of the best Grey Cup games ever played.

Sun photo by Robert Taylor

11: The Double Double

The 1987-88 season started with a Canada Cup and a winning goal for the ages, with Wayne Gretzky setting up Mario Lemieux for the winner in the second overtime against the Soviets. And it ended with the only five-game four-game sweep in Stanley Cup history. It was the Oilers vs. the Boston Bruins in the Stanley Cup final. And the headline in *The Sun* after Game 4 in the old Boston Garden was: "The Game That Never Was." It was the night the lights were supposed to go out on the Boston Bruins, but instead they went out on the Stanley Cup. Left in the dark with the score tied 3-3, the league reached into the Dark Ages to find a rule that required the teams to go back to Edmonton to play Game 4B. The Oilers won 6-3. And when it was over, the highlight was a Gretzky-inspired on-ice team picture which every Stanley Cup winner since has duplicated. But this picture would be special for another reason: it was the last time Gretzky would be on the ice with the Oilers.

RIGHT: The Edmonton Sun's front page says it all: the Oilers had proved the club had staying power, taking the team's fourth Stanley Cup in five years.
BELOW: This impromptu team photo with the Cup marked the last time Wayne Gretzky would be on the ice with the Edmonton Oilers.

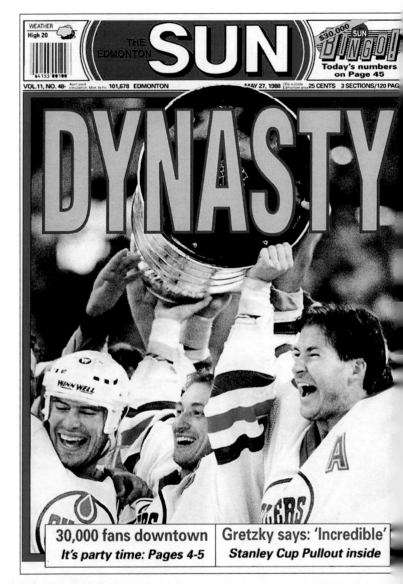

30,000 fans downtown
It's party time: Pages 4-5

Gretzky says: 'Incredible'
Stanley Cup Pullout inside

Sun file photo

Sun file photo

he Oilers clear the bench as they begin to celebrate their fourth Stanley Cup victory.

12: The 1988 Royal Wedding

It was my one scoop during *The Sun* run that I didn't break in the Little Paper That Grew. I broke it on my *Morning Crew* radio gig at CHED at the time. The tip had come in on the cash-for-news-tips line. It had happened after deadline at Earl's Tin Palace and there was no way it was going to last the day, although Gretzky had hoped it might: "My last words to everybody were 'Let's keep it quiet for a while. I guess it kept quiet for about four hours.'" He said he ought to have called the station himself and made

the $1,000 for news tip of the month. Having the scoop on the story made all the difference in the next day's *Sun* coverage. "She said yes," said No. 99 of actress Janet Jones. "It's definite. We're getting married. We were meant to spend our lives together." And so it began. It was called Canada's Royal Wedding. And *The Sun* covered it as such. It was a wonderful wedding and on July 16, 1988, it looked for all the world as if Wayne & Janet & Edmonton would live happily ever after.

Sun photo by Paul Wodehous

Wayne Gretzky waves goodbye as he and Janet prepare to be driven off in their limousine.

13: Minus 99

The Edmonton Sun headline will be remembered almost as long as the day will be remembered: "99 Tears." There was a picture of Wayne Gretzky dabbing his tears. No subhead. And the following: "Pages 2, 3, 4, 5, 6, 10, 11, 18, 19, 23, 30, 36, 37, 38, 39, 40, 41, 42, 43, 46 and 47." Nobody will remember it as a highlight. But if there's one date in Edmonton sports history few will ever forget, it was Aug. 9, 1988 – the day Oilers' owner Peter Pocklington sold No. 99 to the Los Angeles Kings for $18 million. After scoring 583 goals and recording 1,086 assists for 1,669 points in the regular season and adding 81 goals and 171 assists for 252 points in 120 playoff games, setting 43 NHL records, winning eight Hart Trophies, seven Art Ross Trophies, four Stanley Cups, and two Conn Smythe Trophies in nine NHL seasons in Edmonton, Wayne Gretzky was gone.

RIGHT: A choked-up Gretzky manages to give the thumbs-up during the press conference announcing his trade.
BELOW: Oilers general manager Glen Sather takes to the microphone as Gretzky wipes tears away in the background.

Sun photos by Perry Mah

14: The Drive For Five

Life went on. Breaking up was hard to do, but the Oilers managed. Wayne Gretzky came back to play in the All-Star Game in Edmonton, to beat the Oilers in the playoffs and, at the start of his second season in L.A., to break Gordie Howe's record of 1,850 points. But the rest of the story for the rest of the year was the Oilers. They put together one more great year, made it all the way to the 1990 Stanley Cup final against the Boston Bruins and won it a way they'd never won it before. On the road. "We stepped into another era," said Kevin Lowe. "Five Cups!" On the plane ride home Glenn Anderson sat with the Cup strapped in the seat beside him and sang the theme song: "Simply The Best – Better Than All The Rest." And when the Oilers returned home they were given the high-five. "It's like winning it for the first time all over again," said coach John Muckler after the parade around the track at Commonwealth Stadium.

RIGHT: For one last time, the Oilers put together another great year and in 1990 brought the Stanley Cup home.
BELOW: Kevin Lowe, left, Mark Messier, centre, and Jari Kurri hoist the Stanley Cup and acknowledge fans' accolades at Commonwealth Stadium.

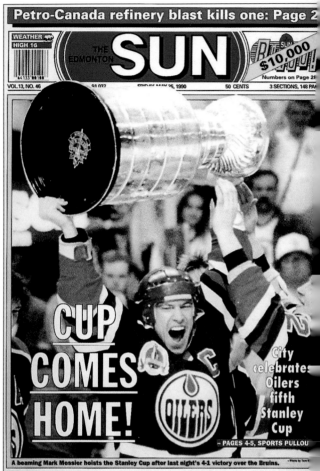

Petro-Canada refinery blast kills one: Page 2

WEATHER
HIGH 16

THE EDMONTON SUN

BINGO $10,000
Numbers on Page 28

VOL.13, NO. 46   91,037   FRIDAY MAY 25, 1990   50 CENTS   3 SECTIONS, 148 PAGES

CUP COMES HOME!

City celebrates Oilers fifth Stanley Cup

– PAGES 4-5, SPORTS PULLOUT

A beaming Mark Messier hoists the Stanley Cup after last night's 4-1 victory over the Bruins.

Sun photo by Tom Braid

134

Sun photo by Perry Mah

Messier and his teammates were mobbed at the Edmonton International Airport on their return home following their Game 5 win against the Boston Bruins – the first league championship won by the Oilers on the road.

15: Kurt Browning

Paris 1989. The Eiffel Tower. Notre Dame. The Louvre. Arc de Triomphe. Champs Elysees. Kurt Browning. OK, Browning was a temporary attraction. The first figure skater to land a quad won his first World Figure Skating Championship and *The Edmonton Sun* was the only Canadian newspaper there. The son of an Albertan mountain guide and outfitter from Caroline, skating out of the Edmonton Royal Glenora, Browning would go on to change the face of figure skating and put hockey, football, baseball and even curling fans, who had previously cringed at the idea of watching figure skating, in front of the TV set. And he'd take this writer on a mystical, magical tour around the world following his career. As wonderful as that first gold medal was in Paris, it was the last one, in his final event, in Prague 1993, which was sweetest. Skating his signature *Casablanca* routine, Browning bounced back from a Lillehammer Olympics disaster and joined American Scott Hamilton as the only four-time world champion since the 1950s.

Sun photo by Perry Mah

Sun photo by Walter Tychnowicz

ABOVE: Kurt Browning poses with his three world championship gold medals in this March 1991 photo. He went on to win a fourth, in Prague in 1993, but Olympic gold eluded him.
LEFT: The pride of Caroline, the town even named a local arena after him.

Browning skated his trademark *Casablanca* **routine, in this January 1994 photo.**

Sun photo by Walter Tychnowicz

Sun photo by Walter Tychnowicz

16: 6.0 For Pure Perfection

Ottavio Cinquanta, the head of the ISU, didn't enjoy the week much. He was booed unmercifully for refusing to allow Kurt Browning to skate in the opening ceremonies because pros are pros and rules are rules. By the end he waved the white flag and Browning and Kristi Yamaguchi were flown in to skate in the closing ceremony of what was otherwise from start to finish a brilliant 1996 World Figure Skating Championship. The ultimate memory maker was Michelle Kwan's win over China's Lu Chen in the women's singles. The two both skated to perfection, both putting up two 6.0s. No woman had ever scored a 6.0 at Worlds before. Canada's Elvis 'The King Is Dead' Stojko crashed and burned in the short program and only the bronze-medal dance team of Shae-Lynn Bourne & Victor Kraatz kept Canada from getting skunked. But when it was over, whether through attendance (sold out start to finish), money ($5.6 million net profit) technical merit or artistic impression, Edmonton had given the world its most successful Worlds ever. "It was an organizational masterpiece," said Canadian skating head David Dore. "It was overwhelming. It was pure perfection."

Sun photo by Jacqui Buchanan

LEFT: Shae-Lynn Bourne and Victor Kraatz were the lone Canadian medallists.
ABOVE: A chagrined Elvis Stojko holds The Sun with the front page headline declaring the near impossibility of his winning the gold.

Sun photo by Christine Vanzella

ISU head Ottavio Cinquanta saved face by finally allowing Kurt Browning to skate in the March 26, 1996 finale.

139

17: S.O.S. – Stay Oilers Stay

Gone were the Winnipeg Jets. Gone were the Quebec Nordiques. And going, going ... People will never know how close the Edmonton Oilers came to being gone. Peter Pocklington, his financial empire crumbling, tried to sell the team to Houston Rockets owner Les Alexander, who came to town and quickly became Less Alexander when he was presented with a location agreement Pocklington had previously signed with Northlands. There was the farce of Michael Largue, a loony without any loonies holding a press conference to announce he wanted to buy the team. But in the end Cal Nichols put together Jim Hole, Bruce Saville and a long list of others with $5 million here and $1 million there to buy the team and save the Oilers. It was only months earlier that many of the same people played a part in keeping the Trappers in town. The Eskimos bought the Trappers, making them both community-owned teams. And suddenly we had a hockey team with 37 owners. No city in the world could claim three pro teams controlled by the community.

Sun photo by Walter Tychnowicz

Houston Rockets owner Les Alexander had to contend with a great deal of press when he came to Edmonton.

Sun photo by Brendon Dlouhy

Oilers investors Bruce Saville, left, Cal Nichols, centre, and Jim Hole celebrate by uncorking a bottle of champagne after a news conference at the Edmonton Convention Centre announcing their offer to purchase the Oilers.

New Yorker Michael Largue arrived in Edmonton to investigate the possibility of buying the Oilers. He was later exposed as a phoney with no money.

Sun photo by Jack Dagley

Sun photo by Christine Vanzella

Even *Baywatch* actress Gena Lee Nolin entered the fray during a visit to the city, showing her support for the campaign to keep the Oilers in Edmonton.

18: Two Much!

It was like they were partners and painted a masterpiece of Olympic drama and history together. At the Nagano Olympics in Japan, Pierre Lueders of Edmonton didn't win the two-man bobsled race. But he won gold. In one of the most incredible events in Olympic and bobsled history, Lueders and Guenther Huber of Italy tied to within 1/100th of a second and were both awarded gold medals. Lueders gained .03 seconds on Huber on the final run to create the tie. "It was amazing. Unbelievable. We drove through all these conditions, all those turns on four different runs and end up tied to the 1/100th of a second," said Lueders who had the fastest of all the single runs. While Lueders himself had enjoyed World Cup titles before and since, it was the only Olympic two-man bobsled gold medal in Canadian history. *The Sun* ran a special printed-at-8-a.m. edition to commemorate the achievement.

Sun photo by Dan Riedlhuber

Pierre Lueders shows off the gold medal he won at Nagano.

19: 1999 Edmonton Brier

Edmonton raised the bar. At the bar. And at the Brier. It was The Last Shootout Of The Century and the 1999 Edmonton Brier left numbers that future Briers would shoot for. Edmonton had played host to the Brier before at the old Edmonton Gardens and at the AgriCom. But this one was at Skyreach Centre and never in its 70-year history had so many people paid to watch. And they had never bought so many drink tokens at the Brier Patch between and after draws. The Edmonton Brier drew 242,887, to break Calgary's 1997 record by 19,565. And at the Brier Patch, Edmonton sold 190,000 Hec Gervais drink tokens to beat Calgary's record of 160,000. Jeff Stoughton and his Buffalo Boys from Manitoba won it. But Territories skip Orest Peech, who went 0-11, put it best: "The support from this city was incredible. It kept me smiling. Because of Edmonton, the whole experience wasn't a disaster."

Sun photo by Walter Tychnowicz

Edmonton crowds like this one, for the opening ceremonies at Skyreach Centre, set attendance records during the 1999 Brier.

Sun photo by Perry Mah

The Manitoba rink, from left, Jeff Stoughton, Jonathan Mead, Garry Van Den Berghe and Doug Armstrong hoist the Labatt Tankard. The Manitoba rink won what was the most successful Brier to date.

Sun photo by Perry Mah

Former Edmonton Oilers great Wayne Gretzky and Edmonton Mayor Bill Smith pose with the sign for Wayne Gretzky Drive Oct. 1, 1999. The city renamed Capilano Drive in Gretzky's honour.

20: The Gretzstravaganza

The temperature was -1 C and snowing when Oct. 1, 1999 arrived and the crowds came to City Hall to view the unveiling of the Wayne Gretzky Drive sign. That same evening the Oilers honoured Gretzky, raising a banner with his number to the ceiling of Skyreach Centre at the Oilers season opener. It was years earlier that Gretzky had come back to have his statue unveiled, a statue he refused to look at in front of Skyreach Centre on any visit until this one. "People are always going to look at me as an Oiler."

Before the banner was unveiled, a replica banner was delivered to Gretzky at centre ice by his special friend Joey Moss, the Oilers dressing room attendant. Gretzky's eyes were wet as the official banner made its trip to the rafters at Skyreach. "I never dreamed of this kind of day," said Gretzky. "My dreams were to make it in the NHL and have my name on the Stanley Cup. I never dreamed of a night like this. It was a wonderful night. Tonight was special. I was an Oiler again." An Oiler forever.

Sun photos by Perry Mah

ABOVE: Gretzky and his pal Joey Moss, the Oilers dressing room attendant, unveil a replica banner before the official banner is raised to the Skyreach rafters.
RIGHT: Gretzky waves to the crowds during the ceremony unveiling the Wayne Gretzky Drive sign.

Sun photo by Walter Tychnowicz

Fans cheered the Canadian team during the opening ceremonies of the 8th IAAF World Championships in Athletics at Commonwealth Stadium. The Edmonton Worlds, in August 2001, marked the first time the event was held in North America.

21: Another World

It was called Edmonton 2001, and it was the eighth IAAF World Championships in Athletics. But it was a first. Never before had the sport that owns the centre ring of the five-ring Olympic circus ever brought its world championships to North America. And Edmonton was left with another treasure chest of memories as the flags of 200 nations flew over Commonwealth Stadium and the city welcomed the world yet again. As track legend Sebastian Coe exclaimed: "Something happened every day." There was stunned disbelief at Marion Jones losing her 100-metre final, the drama of Stacy Dragilla

and Svetlana Feofanova going for gold and a world record at the same time in the pole vault, the freeze frame of Hicham El Guerrouj winning his last 1,500-metre race and legendary Maria Mutola catching Stephanie Graf in a photo finish in the 800. But while a Brit scribe declared the town to be "Deadmonton," in the end, after 10 days of gorgeous blue-sky weather for an event with a total attendance of 400,886 and a declared profit of $10.5 million, it was unanimous that what was achieved here could not have been achieved anywhere else in North America.

Sun photo by Walter Tychnowicz

ABOVE: American runner Marion Jones, No. 830, was beaten by Ukrainian runner Zhanna Pintusevich-Block, No. 799, in the women's 100-metre final Aug. 6, 2001.

LEFT: Pintusevich-Block began celebrating as soon as she crossed the finish line in the 100-metre final.

Sun photo by Perry Mah

RIGHT: Maria Mutola of Mozam-bique, No. 562, put on a finishing kick to pass Stephanie Graf of Austria, No. 35, and Letitia Vriesde of Surinam, No. 756, to take gold in the women's 800-metre event.
BELOW: Hicham El Guerrouj of Morocco collapsed after he won gold in the men's 1,500-metre final.

Sun photo by Perry Mah

Sun photo by Christine Vanzella

Sun photo by Walter Tychnowicz

Gold medal-winning pairs figure skater David Pelletier is hugged by Lt.-Gov. Lois Hole as his partner Jamie Sale smiles during the Pride in Our Olympians Day ceremony at City Hall March 11, 2002.

22: Jamie Sale & David Pelletier

David Pelletier kissed the ice. Jamie Sale, who skated the last two minutes just beaming, threw her arms in the air. They did a double high-five. They had a huge hug. Pelletier threw his hands to his forehead. Sale said, "Oh, my God! Yes!" The crowd chanted "Six! Six! Six!" But the story was "Fix! Fix! Fix." I wrote it on deadline that night: "They were screwed, blued and tattooed and if you want to point the finger at the fixer, it was Miss Marie Reine Le Gougne of France." Bingo! Within days she'd been exposed as the dirty judge. A year earlier, only months after Sale & Pelletier had been put together as a pair, they won the Worlds. This night they won Olympic gold but didn't get it. The Olympics were rocked by the scandal and Sale & Pelletier became worldwide celebrities. Eventually they fixed the fix and gave gold medals to the Edmonton Royal Glenora skaters. And the pair came home to Edmonton and a capacity crowd at Skyreach Centre for A Golden Homecoming.

Sun photos by Darryl Dyck

RIGHT: Jamie Sale and David Pelletier skate
their Love Story routine at the beginning of A
Golden Homecoming, an evening of figure
skating celebrating their Olympic gold medals,
at Skyreach Centre March 12, 2002.
ABOVE: Sale and Pelletier answer questions
during a news conference at the Royal Glenora
Club March 4, 2002. It was the first time the
pair had spoken with the media since returning
home from the 2002 Olympics, held in Salt Lake
City, Utah.

23: The Girls Of Summer

Nobody really knew what to make of the 2002 FIFA U-19 women's world championships before it began. For one thing, it was the inaugural event. And it was teenage girls soccer. But *The Sun* was all over it. And, boy, did it become a story. "Boy Can They Play" was the slogan. And boy, did they steal the hearts of the city and, in the end, the entire country. Christine Sinclair (who won the Golden Boot and the Golden Ball as top scorer and MVP), Kara Lang and gang gave new meaning to the term go-go girls as they went all the way to a golden-goal overtime final against the highly favoured Americans. Commonwealth Stadium was declared a sellout two days before the game and 47,784 sat in the stands to bring the stunning total attendance for six dates in Edmonton to 162,207. The success inspired FIFA boss Sepp Blatter to say: "What they realized here is extraordinary in the 27 years I've witnessed FIFA events. The whole event has been ballistic."

Sun photo by Perry Mah

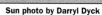

Sun photo by Darryl Dyck

LEFT: Sasha Andrews is mobbed after scoring the winning goal in the penalty kick format, used to decide the winner because Canada and Brazil tied 1-1 following regulation play and two sudden-death overtime periods in their semifinal match Aug. 29, 2002. ABOVE: Lindsay Tarpley scores the winning goal past Canadian goalkeeper Erin McLeod during the 2nd half of extra time of the championship final Sept. 1.

Sun photo by Perry Mah

Kara Lang celebrates after scoring a goal on a penalty kick in the semifinal match against Brazil.

24: Grey Cup Host With The Most

It had never happened before. A team from a Prairie province had never before made it to a Grey Cup game hosted by the team. Twice previously, in 1984 and 1997, Edmonton had been a brilliant host of the Grey Cup. Forced to organize the '97 Grey Cup in nine months, Edmonton drew 60,431. Revenue was a staggering $8,848,000 with a net profit of $3,302,562, most of which the organization used to buy the Edmonton Trappers baseball team. "It's never been done any better," said CFL chairman John Tory. "A Grey Cup has never been that successful. If you had to print a handbook of how to run a Grey Cup, the first three chapters would be Edmonton." But, as was the case in '84, the Eskimos weren't in the game and the game was a dud. In 2002 the Eskimos were in the game. And, while the Eskimos lost it 25-16, it was a game. It was also an event. Shania Twain sang and there was a draw for $6.49 million at halftime. And Edmonton made it bigger and better. With a Grey Cup crowd of 62,531, the Eskimos ended up making a profit of $4,212,869 on the season.

Sun photo by Tom Braid

ABOVE: Crowds watch a fireworks display over Commonwealth Stadium before the Grey Cup game.
RIGHT: Honour guards, firefighter Jim Henderson, left, and paramedic David Maclean, draped in coloured streamers, stand next to the Grey Cup at Edmonton's City Hall as fireworks go off overhead.

Sun photo by Perry Mah

Sun photo by Darryl Dyck

Edmonton Eskimos' John Avery walks off the field following the Eskimos' loss to the Montreal Alouettes. Despite the loss, the 2002 Edmonton Grey Cup was an undisputed success.

25: Ferbey Writes Brier History

Edmonton has produced some of the greatest curling rinks ever. Matt Baldwin won three Briers and the Hec Gervais, Pat Ryan and Kevin Martin rinks all won a pair – Baldwin and Ryan managing to win back-to-back Briars. But in Halifax, in the spring of 2003, Randy Ferbey's fab foursome, featuring Dave Nedohin, Scott Pfeifer and Marcel Rocque, did something that no other curlers had ever accomplished. They won three in a row. Even the famed Ernie Richardson rink of Saskatchewan, which won four, didn't win three in a row. And for Ferbey, who played third for Ryan, it was an unprecedented fifth Brier title. To make it absolutely perfect, the rink was absolutely perfect, going through both the provincial finals and the Brier undefeated. A second straight world championship, won in Winnipeg, was the icing on the cake.

Sun photos by Darryl Dyck

Randy Ferbey throws a rock in the final game of the 2003 Alberta Men's Curling Championship. His rink went on to represent Alberta in the Brier.

• • •

So there it is. Twenty-five great moments in sport in *The Edmonton Sun*. Thank goodness they didn't ask me to rank them in order.

It would be ridiculous to expect the next 25 years to produce a list that could compare. Then again, this is Edmonton. This is the City of Champions & Championships.

The 2003 Nokia Brier champions, from left, lead Marcel Rocque, skip Randy Ferbey, third Dave Nedohin and second Scott Pfeifer pose for a photograph in front of the City of Champions sign after returning from Halifax March 3, 2003.

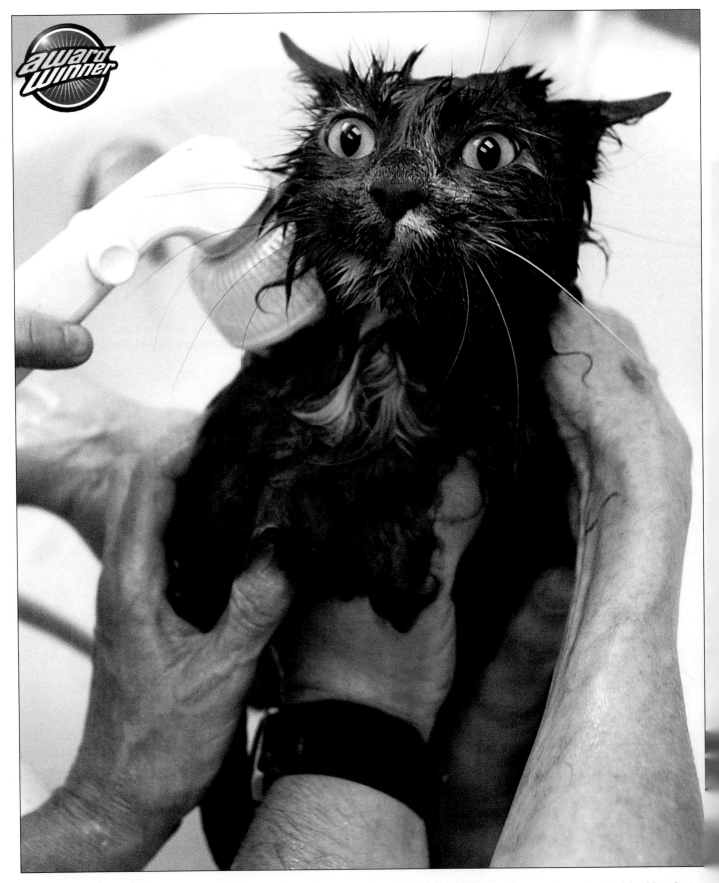

Alhi, a house cat, is held by three sets of hands as she's rinsed at a dog, cat and car wash at a city veterinary hospital in this July 6, 2002 photo by Darryl Dyck. The image won a Canadian Press Enterprise Photo of the Month Award.

CHAPTER EIGHT
Politics

Edmonton Friends of the North co-chairman Randy Lawrence, right, gives the finger to Economic Development Minister Peter Elzinga at a press conference in Athabasca announcing the approval of the Al-Pac pulp mill. This Walter Tychnowicz photo, taken Dec. 20, 1990, was given an honourable mention in the spot news photography category of Sun Media's Dunlop Awards.

157

John Larter

The funny guys

It's been said the pen is mightier than the sword.

That has certainly been proven true given the razor-sharp pens wielded over the years by *Edmonton Sun* editorial cartoonists.

Since its inception in 1978, *The Sun* has been blessed with a bevy of talented cartoonists who've used their pens to lampoon politicians of all stripes.

The paper's first was Swift Current, Sask., native John

Larter who started his career at the *Lethbridge Herald* and began entertaining *Edmonton Sun* readers with his witty work in 1978.

In March 1980, Brit native Yardley Jones joined *The Sun* after toiling for our cross-town rival, the *Edmonton Journal*.

Before that, the former Liverpool resident worked at the now-defunct *Toronto Telegram* before joining the *Toronto Sun*.

Yardley Jones

Victor Roschkov

National Newspaper Award-winning cartoonist Victor Roschkov brought his pen, ink and poignant wit to *The Edmonton Sun* in March 1984.

When he was a commercial artist in London, Ont., Roschkov drew caricatures of co-workers – and his work was so good he was encouraged to turn his attention to doing caricatures of politicians.

He landed his first full-time editorial cartooning job at the *Windsor Star,* where he worked for five years before joining the *Toronto Star* for six years.

Fred Curatolo has been *The Edmonton Sun*'s political cartoonist since 1989, having come here from Ontario after working three years at the *Brampton Guardian*.

The self-described "converted westerner" has been drawing since age three and had his first editorial cartoon published in *The Toronto Sun* in 1983.

Curatolo's work has proved so popular it has been featured in every major English-language newspaper in Canada as well as in scores of community newspapers nationwide.

Fred Curatolo

Mavericks And Leaders

For more than 30 years the Progressive Conservative party has ruled provincial politics in Alberta.

And it all started with the 1971 election victory by the Tories under Peter Lougheed over the Social Credit party, winning 49 of 75 provincial seats.

His shoes were filled years later by former CFL football player Don Getty, a man Lougheed encouraged to lead the party.

When Getty saw the writing on the wall as his popularity waned, he stepped aside for what would become the Ralph Revolution.

Former Calgary mayor Ralph Klein entered the fray to put his unique brand on provincial politics.

Amid all of that there were other political rumblings out of Wild Rose Country.

In 1982 Gord Kesler became the province's first-ever elected separatist, winning a byelection in the southern Alberta riding of Olds-Didsbury for the Western Canada Concept (WCC) party. He lasted just one term.

Preston Manning rose to the national stage out of Calgary to head what became the Reform Party of Canada.

When that party decided it needed a better chance of winning seats nationwide, its members voted to change its moniker to the Canadian Alliance party.

Joe Clark waves from the podium at his campaign headquarters in Spruce Grove on election night, Feb. 18, 1980, the night his party lost the federal election and he effectively lost his position as Canada's prime minister.

It ditched Manning as leader shortly after in favour of former Klein cabinet minister Stockwell Day, who was a much-touted, popular young leader for several months but quickly fell out of favour with the Canadian public and media.

Day headed the Canadian Alliance just two years before losing a leadership race to Stephen Harper.

While neither Day nor Manning ever realized their dream to govern, fellow Albertan Joe Clark did as leader of the federal Tories.

The High River-born Clark served as Tory PM from June 4, 1979 to March 2, 1980.

But it was Calgary-born lawyer Lougheed who was the first of a string of popular conservative politicians in the last three decades.

Lougheed was seemingly almost a god in voters' minds, winning huge majority governments in 1975, 1979 and 1982.

He was best known for his ongoing wars with the federal government, particularly over energy.

He long fought for better energy prices for the province and backed up demands by cutting oil production.

As the province's wealth expanded in the 1970s, Lougheed's government spent money on parks, new hospitals and medical research facilities.

The money poured in so well for a time that

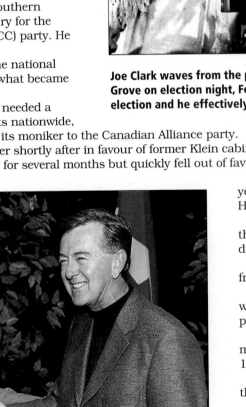

Sun photo by Brendon Dlouhy

Reform party Leader Preston Manning, right, mugs for the cameras as he and Conservative party Leader Clark shake hands Sept. 11, 1999 after a policy conference aimed at uniting the political right in Canada.

Lougheed's government set up the Alberta Heritage Savings Trust Fund to stockpile billions of dollars from oil and gas revenues.

But Lougheed was seen as a failure by some in representing Alberta on the national scene, particularly on the energy front.

While he fought the federally imposed national energy program (NEP) for a time, he wound up inking an oil-pricing agreement with Prime Minister Pierre Trudeau and toasting it with champagne.

It was based on the premise that oil would hit $75 a barrel by 1986 – but prices collapsed.

Albertans with some sympathy for separatist sentiments also do not remember Lougheed fondly for his support for repatriating the nation's Constitution in 1981.

Lougheed stepped down as premier in 1985 and went back to private business.

He returned to the political arena briefly in 2002 to help the province fight the Kyoto accord, which calls for dramatic reductions in greenhouse gases.

Sun photo by Bill Brennan

ABOVE: Premier Peter Lougheed rides a horse in the Calgary Stampede Parade in this July 6, 1980 photo. LEFT: Lougheed looks pensive in this February 1983 photo taken during a press conference to announce that he would not run for the leadership of the federal Progressive Conservative party.

Sun photo by Paul Wodehouse

Sun photo by Gorm Larsen

Premier Don Getty seemed plagued by a string of events and circumstances that combined to send his popularity plummeting.

Getty followed in Lougheed's giant footsteps but was never as personally popular as his predecessor or as popular as Klein, who took over when Getty stepped down.

With treasurer Dick Johnston calling the financial shots, Getty's government put the province into debt for the first time since the Great Depression.

It was an attempt to spend the province into some sort of recovery in the wake of the recession brought on by the federal NEP and the collapse of oil prices.

Johnston brought in six deficit budgets in a row in Alberta.

To compound Getty's woes, his government was stung by a whole series of bad loans and loan guarantees it made to large corporations – including multinational pulp and paper companies.

Getty was further stung by the collapse of the Principal Group, a trust and investment company that failed and left scores of investors out millions of dollars.

An enduring image of the former premier was of him on a golf course in the wake of the failure of the government-regulated company.

Reporters trying to reach Getty that day were told he was

working out of the office.

Getty's personal popularity as Progressive Conservative leader received its toughest blow in 1989 when he lost the race in his own riding in the March provincial election.

The defeat came even as the Tories scored a sixth consecutive majority government.

The opposition scored some gains, notably the New Democrats who elected 16 MLAs. The support for the NDs was so strong locally, this city earned the nickname Redmonton.

Getty's personal defeat came at the hands of Liberal Percy Wickman, a paraplegic former city councillor.

"It's shocking," said Wickman after he beat the horse race-loving Getty by a nose – 8,355 votes to 8,003 in Edmonton Whitemud.

Most pundits observed Getty's campaign got off to a bad start when he made a joke about wife-beating at a news conference.

Weeks before that news conference, *Sun* columnist Don Wanagas surmised the premier might not wear a car seat belt as mandated by law. He wrote that Getty might be a closet seat-belt abuser.

Getty called out to the columnist at the election kickoff news conference, saying, "I may whack my kids, beat my wife, but I've never abused a seat belt."

Other observers felt the crippling blow to Getty came because he had refused to debate Wickman during the campaign.

Sun photo by Doug Shanks

An enduring image of Premier Getty was this photo of him on the golf course during the collapse of the Principal Group. Reporters trying to reach him were told he was working out of the office.

The Grit made headlines by instead staging a mock debate with a stuffed chicken.

Getty wound up being elected later in Stettler during a byelection. He stayed on until 1992.

Sun photo by Dan Riedlhuber

Nancy Betkowski said goodbye to politics shortly after losing the provincial Tory leadership race to Ralph Klein. Here, the two shake hands following the March 7, 1993 announcement of her departure from public life. She returned to the provincial scene – as Nancy MacBeth – as leader of the Alberta Liberal party in 1998.

A bitter battle for the party leadership ensued, with dark-horse candidate Klein beating former cabinet colleague Nancy Betkowski in 1992.

That essentially marked the start of what he called a new approach to government – one that became known as the Ralph Revolution.

Klein was facing a $3.42-billion government deficit and an accumulated debt that was seven times as high.

His government undertook a drastic series of spending cuts.

Civil servants, including teachers, saw their wages rolled back.

Many aspects of the government – including liquor sales and motor vehicle registration – were privatized and legislation was passed to outlaw deficit budgets in Alberta.

Klein likened it all to getting a house in order and promised there would be no more loans made to businesses, a practice that got the previous Tory government in trouble. "We are out of the business of being in business," Klein vowed.

What his government was attempting to create was something called the Alberta Advantage – a province with lower taxation than others and an affinity for free enterprise.

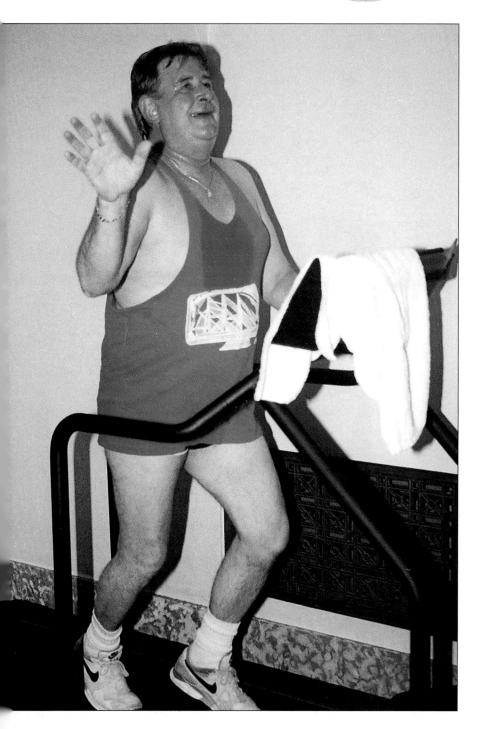

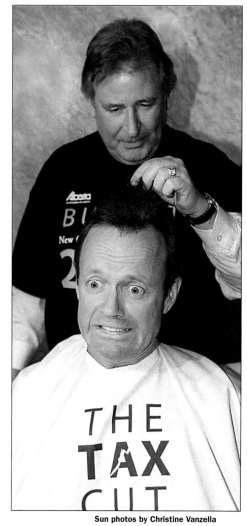

Sun photos by Christine Vanzella

LEFT: Premier Ralph Klein battled a heavy provincial debt while at the same time contending with a burgeoning waistline. The premier is seen Sept. 12, 1996 as he follows his daily regimen of running three miles in 24 minutes.
ABOVE: Klein takes a bit off the top for Stockwell Day in this Feb. 23, 2000 photo. Day, then the provincial treasurer, went on to become leader of the Alliance party.

Klein's Tories wiped out the deficit within three years and the accumulated debt of almost $20 billion was reduced to less than $5 billion in about 10 years.

The roly-poly premier's popularity reached new heights in the March 2001 provincial election when even so-called 'Redmonton' opted to vote Tory in many ridings.

"Welcome to Ralph's World," Klein beamed while making his victory speech.

It certainly was his world after that night.

Klein's crew dominated the former Liberal stronghold in Edmonton by gaining eight seats in the city.

That included dethroning Liberal Leader Nancy MacBeth

(nee Betkowski) in her riding of Edmonton-McClung.

The Liberals wound up winning seven seats, down from 15. The New Democrats retained a pair of seats.

Later, Klein crowed: "This success is beyond my wildest dreams. Our people in Edmonton have done an incredible job representing the PC party's vision to the people of the Capital Region. Our government will do what it can to help the city of Edmonton."

Since then, City of Edmonton politicians have repeatedly questioned just how much the province has done for them. They complain that some provincial services have been downloaded on to cities and estimate Edmonton shells out

$88 million annually to pay for services that should be borne by the province.

Klein also ran into trouble in the court of public opinion, making national headlines when he showed up unannounced at an Edmonton homeless shelter just before Christmas 2001 after drinking with friends.

Klein claimed to have been "in very good spirits" when he paid an early morning visit to the Herb Jamieson Centre at 105A Avenue and 101 Street.

Some of the residents claimed those "very good spirits" didn't translate into the premier being friendly.

They claimed he got into a heated argument with some, asked them why they didn't have jobs and threw money at them.

Some of the men he spoke to there said Klein was unsteady on his feet and slurring his words.

An initial statement by the premier claimed the purpose of the visit was to "chat with residents and find out what their situations are like."

A couple of days later the premier admitted to having a drinking problem.

"I drink too much from time to time," Klein told reporters. "I'm going to resolve to control and curb my drinking.

"I have the support of my wife, my family, my caucus and my friends."

The premier's personal popularity didn't wane in Alberta after the shelter incident, but many questioned his government's direction on spending.

Sun photo by Brendon Dlouhy

Klein stands in the legislative assembly sporting a native headdress as he speaks before the Tories tabled the First Nations Sacred Ceremonial Objects Repatriation Act March 1, 2000.

The formerly fiscally conservative Klein Tories earned barbs from several quarters for launching a spending spree after his 2001 re-election.

Expenditures in the 2001 budget were 22% higher than the previous year.

In 2002, 75% of the government's ministries spent more than what they were initially allotted in that year's budget.

That all came amid large provincial surpluses.

Since Klein's Tories declared their first surplus in 1994-95, their cumulative surpluses totalled $20.7 billion by the spring of 2003.

CHAPTER NINE
Music, Music, Music...

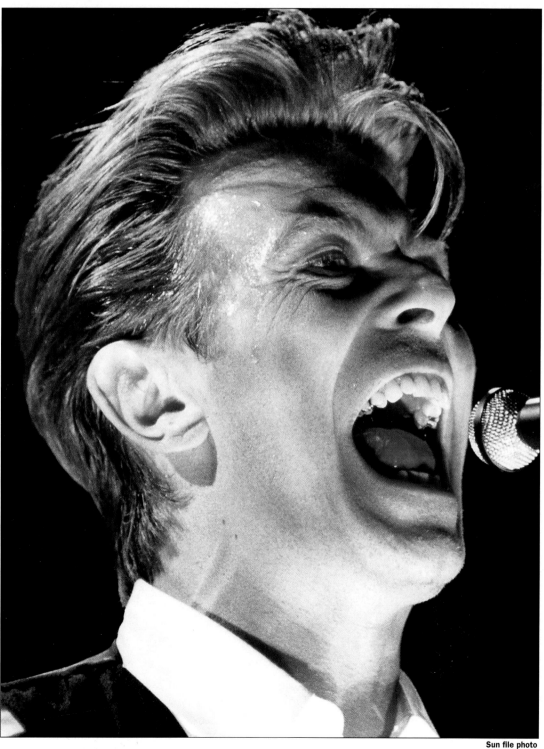

Sun file photo

David Bowie cuts loose at Northlands March 12, 1990, on his Sound and Vision tour.

Sun photo by Dan Riedlhuber

Mick Jagger belts out a tune while Ron Wood plays guitar. The Rolling Stones sold out two concerts at Commonwealth Stadium in October 1999.

The Stage Is Set...

Ask any music promoter and they will admit it is sometimes a challenge to get top acts to perform in Edmonton.

That is partly because of where we are geographically and the lack of a number of direct flights to other North American cities.

It is complicated these days by the fact most touring acts get paid in American dollars and can make more of the green stuff south of Alberta's border.

But this city has enjoyed numerous memorable musical shows in the last 25 years, being blessed with both a large hockey arena and Commonwealth Stadium – the nation's largest-capacity public venue.

Soon after *The Edmonton Sun* began publishing in 1978, promoters lured three major acts for a rock festival.

Those bands just happened to be among the hottest of their era: Heart, Eddie Money and Peter Frampton.

Those same early years at what was then known as the Coliseum saw scintillating performances by some of the top acts of the time, including The Who, the Kinks, Queen, the Police and Alice Cooper.

In later years the building that does dual duty as a hockey rink would be the site of memorable musical acts including Fleetwood Mac, Elton John, the Eagles, John Mellencamp, the Tragically Hip, Garth Brooks and Shania Twain.

A few blocks away, the cavernous Commonwealth Stadium was built for athletes in 1978 but has hosted plenty of musicians since then.

The biggest name to play there in the early days was David Bowie, who performed in 1983 and helped put the venue on the map for American promoters.

Since then tens of thousands of people have turned up to thrill to shows, such as the two sold-out performances by the Rolling Stones in October 1999.

Among the other big-draw acts to entertain at Commonwealth have been U2, the Backstreet Boys, Pink Floyd and artists who played there at Lilith Fair in 1999 – including Sheryl Crow, Sarah McLachlan and the Dixie Chicks.

Sun photo by Perry Mah

Shania Twain in concert, in what is now Skyreach Centre, July 3, 1998.

169

Sun photo by Robert Taylor

Sun photo by Tom Braid

Sun photo by Christine Vanzella

TOP LEFT: Reba McEntire was in town in October 1998.
BOTTOM LEFT: Adam Gregory croons to some young fans during a CD
launch party at Cook County Saloon in July 2002.
ABOVE: Garth Brooks in concert, playing the first of three sold-out
dates in August 1996.

Sun photo by Robert Taylor

Nickelback frontman Chad Kroeger rocks Skyreach in this Jan. 26, 2002 photo. The Alberta-born musician told delirious home-town fans how happy he was to be headlining at a venue where he had seen so many of his musical heroes play.

Sun photo by Perry M

Sun photo by Dan Riedlhuber

ABOVE: Bono, on his arrival at the Edmonton International Airport June 13, 1997, was kissed by fan Carmen Chumulka.
TOP RIGHT: Terri Clark at Big Valley Jamboree, near Camrose, on Aug. 3, 1996.
RIGHT: Ricky Martin in concert March 14, 2000.

Sun photo by Robert Taylor

Sun photo by Perry Mah

Britney Spears sang and danced her way into Edmontonians' hearts during her June 22, 1999 concert at Skyreach Centre.

Sun photo by Preston Brownschlaigle

Steve Tyler and Aerosmith played to a very full, very loud, very appreciative crowd at Skyreach Centre Oct. 31, 2001.

Thank you for buying
Morning Glory

We appreciate your support and your interest in The Edmonton Sun. To help celebrate 25 years in Edmonton, we are going to give $2,500 to one lucky reader of this book. All you have to do is clip the coupon below, fill it out and send it to:

25th Anniversary Great Cash Giveaway
The Edmonton Sun
#250, 4990 92 Ave.
Edmonton, Alberta
T6B 3A1

- -

THE EDMONTON
SUN

5th Anniversary Great
Cash Giveaway

Name:

Address:

Phone:

Name: _ _ _ _ _ _ _ _ _ _ _ _ _ _ _

Address: _ _ _ _ _ _ _ _ _ _ _ _ _
_ _ _ _ _ _ _ _ _ _ _ _ _
_ _ _ _ _ _ _ _ _ _ _ _ _
_ _ _ _ _ _ _ _ _ _ _ _ _

Phone: _ _ _ _ _ _ _ _ _ _ _ _ _

Kids!

*Here's a chance to win a guided tour of The Edmonton Sun with Digger Jr.,
as well as some cool prizes worth $250. Simply colour Digger Jr. and send the
picture to the address below and you will be eligible to win.*

The Edmonton Sun Digger Jr. Contest
#250, 4990 92 Ave.
Edmonton, Alberta
T6B 3A1